YOUTH UNEMPLOYMENT

YOUTH
UNEMPLOYMENT

MICHAEL P JACKSON

CROOM HELM
London ● Sydney ● Dover, New Hampshire

©1985 Michael Jackson
Croom Helm Ltd, Provident House, Burrell Row,
Beckenham, Kent BR3 1AT
Croom Helm Australia Pty Ltd, First Floor,
139 King Street, Sydney, NSW 2001, Australia

British Library Cataloguing in Publication Data

Jackson, Michael P.
    Youth unemployment.
    1. Youth—Employment—Great Britain
    2. Unemployment—Great Britain
    I. Title
    331.3'4137941   HD6276.G7

    ISBN 0-7099-1453-9

Croom Helm, 51 Washington Street, Dover,
New Hampshire 03820, USA

Library of Congress Cataloging in Publication Data

Jackson, Michael Peart.
    Youth unemployment.

    Bibliography: p.
    Includes index.
    1. Youth—Employment—Great Britain. 2. Unemployment
—Great Britain. I. Title.
HD6276.G7J33   1985   331.3'4137941   84-29332
ISBN 0-7099-1453-9

Printed and bound in Great Britain by
Biddles Ltd, Guildford and King's Lynn

CONTENTS

LIST OF TABLES

PREFACE

This book is designed as an introduction to the problems of youth unemployment and the policy response to them. It is based on a recognition that these issues need to be viewed with a knowledge of the contributions that can be made from a variety of different disciplines, including sociology, economics, politics and social policy. It is recognised that few claim mastery of all these subjects and it is written with this in mind.

I am indebted to colleagues for their help and advice. I am particularly indebted to Dorothy Anderson for her work with the preparation of the book.

INTRODUCTION

The sustained rise in the level of unemployment in recent years, has meant that the topic has become a major cause for comment and concern. However, while concern has been shown for all who are unable to find work, most concern has been shown about the young. Sir Raymond Pennock's comment that 'unemployment bites deeply, but bites especially with the young'[1] has been echoed by many. It is not just that the young are often seen as innocent victims, it is also that the young are frequently seen as the most vulnerable and the group for whom the experience of unemployment is likely to have the most serious and lasting impact.

Governments in Britain have reacted to the rise in the level of youth unemployment, and the growing concern about its consequences, mainly by introducing a variety of "special employment measures". The first of these, Community Industry, the Job Creation Programme and the Work Experience Programme were introduced between 1972 and 1976. The most recent, like the Youth Training Scheme, mark a significant departure from earlier endeavours but nevertheless retain also an important continuity. The departure is in the emphasis on training as opposed to job creation, the continuity is in the reliance on targetted employment programmes rather than more general reflationary policies.

The rise in the level of youth unemployment, and the development of special employment measures, has been accompanied by an expansion in the role of the Manpower Services Commission. Since its introduction in 1972 the MSC has become one of the most influential government agencies. Its influence is reflected in the size of its budget and staff and the way in which it has been able to assume a dominant role in training and education for young people over 16 years of age who do not seek to enter the higher education system.

Discussion of youth unemployment, its causes, consequences and the measures most appropriate for dealing with it, has raised many points of conflict and at times inconsistencies. For example, there are major differences over the causes of youth unemployment: are the schools or the young themselves to blame; is it the level of wages young people demand; or is youth unemployment largely a reflection of the overall economic problems? Similarly, there are important differences over the interpretation of evidence about the consequences of youth unemployment: is youth unemployment a major economic disaster for the unemployed themselves or have the economic problems largely been overcome by the provision of state benefits; what is the link between youth unemployment and crime, ill health, and suicide; and to what extent is youth unemployment really the cause of social unrest, and to what extent, therefore, does it constitute a threat to the political system? Again, despite the continuity in policy emphasis between governments of different political eomplexions, there have been many disagreements over the detail of policy proposals: have job creation schemes and training programmes offered young people an experience that will be useful when later competing in the labour market, or have such schemes simply been cosmetic devices primarily designed to reduce the unemployment figures; to what extent have special employment measures led to the creation of genuinely new employment opportunities or have they been used largely as a way of subsidising jobs that would have been filled anyway?

The debates over such questions are complex partly because of the number of different often overlapping opinions that are held. They are also complex because they take in research from a variety of different disciplines. Politics, economics, social policy, psychology and sociology clearly all have a claim on some of the issues under consideration. The list could easily be lengthened. Few who are interested in the area, though, are likely to claim mastery of all of these disciplines, let alone with a longer list.

Introduction

The aim of this book is to examine the area
and the debates and to look at the policy adopted
to try to deal with the problem. The background
to the policies will be examined, as well as the
policies themselves, their effectiveness and their
implications.

The first substantive chapter looks at why
youth unemployment has been seen, and continues to
be seen, as a cause for concern. The consequences of unemployment both for the individuals
directly involved and for society in general are
examined. It is argued that attention needs to
be paid to both of these areas if the motives behind policy measures are to be fully understood;
in other words social policy cannot be seen simply
as a reflection of the compassion policy makers
feel for disadvantaged groups in society.

The second chapter provides part of the essential background for the later discussion; an
analysis of the major trends in youth unemployment
over recent years. It is shown that youth unemployment, like unemployment more generally, has
increased dramatically since the mid 1970s. In
many ways the trends in youth unemployment have
followed the more general lead; nevertheless
youth unemployment has not simply been a mirror
image of the more general position. Young people
seem to have suffered particularly badly in the
early years of the recession. Although few sections of society have been able to escape the effects of unemployment altogether, unemployment
clearly has an uneven incidence.

The third chapter considers a number of different explanations for the level of youth unemployment. It is pointed out that the weight of
evidence suggests that youth unemployment needs to
be seen primarily as a reflection of the general
economic climate rather than as the result of anything more specifically related to the young themselves. Nevertheless, it is clear that many of
the recent policy initiatives are based on different assumptions; in particular, that in part
the problems seen are the result of the inadequate
preparation of the young for the world of work by
the traditional educational system and young
people pricing themselves out of jobs by demanding
high wages.

The following three chapters look in some detail at the policy initiatives. Chapter four
reviews the initiatives that have been taken to

try to deal with youth unemployment, including the use of subsidies, job creation schemes, training and attempts to reduce the size of the active labour force. Trends are identified, in particular the increasing use of training and the decreasing use of job creation, especially for the younger age ranges.

Chapter five examines some of the reasons why the initiatives have been taken, centring on the claims and concerns expressed by politicians and individuals particularly influential in policy making debates. The complexity of the policy making process is stressed and it is argued that no one set of concerns can be seen to have dominated thinking. Chapter six moves on to look at the implications of the policy initiatives. Evidence on the extent to which the policy measures have met explicit objectives is reviewed as well the debate over the less explicit implications of some of the measures.

Chapter seven highlights two issues. The first is an evaluation of the general policy direction, the use of special employment measures to deal with the problems of youth unemployment. Some scepticism is expressed about whether special employment measures, especially the range currently available, are likely to be able to have more than a marginal effect on the problem. The second is to point to some of the implications of the growth and development of the role of the Manpower Services Commission as the body most directly responsible for the implementation of policy in this area. The implications of the rise in the influence of the Commission for the direction of education and training are given particular prominence.

In the concluding chapter some of the earlier themes and strands are drawn together. It is argued that the policy adopted towards youth unemployment in the mid 1970s was the result, in part, of a view that the problem was a short term one, in part, of a view that action to show that the government was doing something to deal with the problem, thus showing its concern (which was essential for the labour governments relations with the trade unions) and in part of a view that youth unemployment held major dangers for society. Later policy on youth unemployment has been based on a some similar but also some different assumptions. One the one hand, the as-

Introduction

sumptions about the political importance of youth
unemployment have continued, and if anything have
been reinforced, and the assumptions about the
social implications of youth unemployment remain
but are no longer as dominant in government
circles. On the other hand youth unemployment is
no longer seen as a short term phenomenon, but
more importantly particular assumptions have been
made about the causes of youth unemployment with
particular emphasis being placed on the effect of
the level of wages and the defects in the educational system. The evidence reviewed in earlier
chapters is recalled to see to what extent the
assumptions underlying policy can be supported.

Notes

1. Quoted in the Times, 11 November 1980

Chapter One

YOUTH UNEMPLOYMENT: A CAUSE FOR CONCERN

Unemployment has become one of the most, if not
the most, important item on the political
agenda.   Later, the way that unemployment has
risen, particularly amongst young people, will be
examined.   For the moment, though, the aim is to
determine why unemployment amongst the young has
been seen as a particular cause for concern.   The
focus, first, will be on the problems that unemployment is believed to cause for the young people
directly affected, and then later, on the consequences for society in general.   Such a division, to a degree, is arbitrary and many points
that need to be discussed straddle the two categories.   Nevertheless, the division is useful in
that it serves to stress the two major sources of
concern.

Consequences For The Individual

Popular discussion of unemployment frequently assumes that the worst economic consequences for the
individual have been alleviated by the provision
of state financial aid.   Redundancy payments, insurance benefits and Supplementary Benefits are
widely believed to cushion the effect of unemployment and, of course, do so to a certain extent.   However, it is clear that for most people
unemployment still has serious economic consequences.   A Department of Health and Social
Security study[1] of unemployed men has shown that
in most cases unemployment is accompanied by a
significant reduction in income.   In their sample, one in five families found that their incomes
fell by at least a half, and in about 60 per cent
of cases incomes when unemployed were no more than

Youth Unemployment: A Cause for Concern

80 per cent of what they had been when in work. Unemployment is clearly associated with poverty. In two thirds of all the cases in the DHSS sample incomes when unemployed were within ten per cent of the Supplementary Benefit level. It is also important to remember that in the case of young people many who face unemployment are unable to claim insurance benefits or redundancy pay, because they have not built up the necessary contribution or because they do not have a long enough work record. Further, school leavers are not able to claim Supplementary Benefit when unemployed for the first three months after they have left school.

It is frequently argued as well that the economic consequences of unemployment are cushioned, in particular for the young, not just by state financial aid but also by help from family and friends. Help may take the form of subsidised or free accommodation or a loan. In practice, rising unemployment has meant that in many cases more than one member of a family has been directly affected and the assumptions that have been made about the help that family and friends are able to give the young unemployed may have to be revised. However, even if family and friends are able to offer young people financial help the independence that goes with a wage will be lost with unemployment.

It is clear that the loss of income resulting from unemployment spins over into other areas. Social activities may be affected: frequently the unemployed no longer have the financial resources to enable them to maintain their previous pattern of social activities. This is important in its own right but also because it may cut off the unemployed person from contacts and sources of information that might be useful for gaining employment in the future. The longer unemployment lasts the worse these effects become.

The main concern surrounding the effects of unemployment on the young people directly affected, though, has centred not on the economic but on the social consequences. There is an extensive literature, for example, on the consequences for social relationships and family life. One recent survey noted how young people are often particularly worried by the effect of unemployment on friendship patterns. One young person was reported as having said: 'When I was at school I used to have loads of friends. Now a lot of them...have got jobs and you tend to lose contact. I've become lonely...I do get terribly depressed at times. I think I'll end it all, but I haven't got the nerve.'[2] A number of other people interviewed in the same survey noted 'that any social life they did have tended to revolve around other people in similar circumstances and this formed a separate structure divorced from the mainstream of social activity. Unemployment also led to a loss of social status. Several respondents noted that other people tended to view them as scroungers and "ne'er-do-wells".'[3] Another survey of unemployment in a Northern British town[4] highlighted the effect of unemployment on family relationships. It showed how unemployment frequently led to arguments within the family over 'little things' and 'rows about money and the children'. In still other studies[5] it has been shown how unemployed men who have been used to assuming the role of provider but can no longer do so find adjustment difficult and view their 'social world' as more threatening.

Another recurring theme in the literature on the social consequences of unemployment stresses the way in which the unemployed frequently become apathetic and resigned to their state. Such a view was commonly expressed by studies of unemployment in the inter-war years: for example, one study[6] told how the unemployed eventually become 'fatalistic' and 'adapt to their new state but with a narrow scope' and a 'broken attitude.' More recent studies have echoed such findings. A study by Donovan and Oddy[7] of unemployed 16 year olds suggested that many were emotionally disturbed and had a low self esteem. Another by Miller[8] found that a significant number of unemployed young people were resigned to never working.

It has been argued that in some cases the 'apathy' and 'fatalism' can lead to depression and even suicide. The studies by Donovan and Oddy and Miller both suggested that unemployed young people frequently suffered long periods of depression and Miller also referred to suicidal feelings in the case of some of his respondents. In fact a number of studies have looked specifically at the relationship between unemployment and suicide. One such study[9] suggested that a one per cent increase in the level of unemployment leads to a 4.1 per cent increase in suicide in the subsequent fifth year. Another study[10] has suggested that unemployed young people are more likely than others to report feelings of depression and suicide, while a third[11] has not only confirmed the strong link between unemployment and attempted suicide (in this study unemployed men were found to be eleven times more likely to attempt suicide than employed men) but also showed a relationship between attempted suicide and the duration of unemployment (in one of the years looked at the proportion of men out of work for more than a year attempting suicide was more than twice that for men out of work for less than a year). It needs to be recorded, though, that these and other similar studies have found it more difficult to establish the nature of the relationship between unemployment and suicide, as opposed to simply noting the association between the two variables, and as a result, have been the subject of considerable debate.

It is also important to record that despite general concern about the social consequences of unemployment a number of authors have tried to challenge the assumption that unemployment is necessarily seen by everyone as significantly worse than work. Pahl argues that it is 'quite wrong to imagine that all men who become unemployed thereby lose the central prop of their social and psychological wellbeing.' Some unemployed are able to find interests away from the world of work: 'students of working class culture have documented the out of work arenas for personal achievement in allotments, brass bands and pigeon keeping.'[12] Similarly Roberts[13] has argued that some young people may be accepting unemployment voluntarily because the only alternative is "boring" and "meaningless" work. Others[14] have argued that because of the prolonged high levels of unemployment there is now little stigma attached to being unemployed after school, and Brinkmann[15] has suggested that young people are better able to deal with the problems unemployment causes for social relationships, though other studies[16] have drawn this assumption into question.

It needs to be stressed, however, that such comments are meant to balance what their authors see as unacceptable generalised contrasts between work and unemployment. In many ways the challenge is directed more at the assumptions about the attractions of work than about the problems caused by unemployment. Pahl stresses, for instance, that he does 'not wish to create a counter-myth of the happy unemployed creative person'.[17]

The extensive literature on the social/ psychological effects of unemployment has clear links with the discussion of the association between unemployment and ill health. There is a wealth of research[18] which shows that the unemployed suffer more from ill health than those in work. For example, data from the General Household Survey[19] shows that in 1976 the proportion of males reporting a long standing illness was about 40 per cent higher for those unemployed than for those in work: if 'limiting' long term illnesses are looked at then reporting by the unemployed was 80 per cent higher than by those in work. Other researchers have pointed more directly to the link between unemployment and mortality. One of the most frequently quoted (but also one of the most frequently criticised methodologically) is that by Brenner[20] where he uses a time lag (of up to 15 years in certain instances) to show the association between unemployment and mortality.

There is little doubt, then, that unemployment is associated with ill health. However, the nature of the association is far from clear. It may be that unemployment because of its economic and social consequences (poverty, increased stress) can be said to 'cause' ill health. On the other hand there are other possibilities. It may be that the causal link is in the opposite direction: that is, ill health causes unemployment. Similarly it may be that the unemployed had low incomes when in work and live in poor housing conditions, both of which help to explain ill health.

A recent study of unemployment and ill health by the Department of Health and Social Security[21] attempted to disentangle some of these explanations by following through a group of unemployed men and seeking information on their health on a number of occasions. The authors of the research report suggested that 'if unemployment does adversely affect health the effect appears to be small during the first year of unemployment'.[22] However, as the authors of that report acknowledge their work does not foreclose debate on this issue. They only considered the position for a year after initial registration (and others have suggested that a more substantial time lag needs to be allowed for) and their sample of continuously unemployed was relatively small.

Other researchers have suggested a clearer causal link between a specific aspect of ill health and unemployment. Banks and Jackson[23] in their work on minor psychological disorders suggest that there is firmer evidence in this case that unemployment leads to psychological disorders rather than vice versa. However, generally much work still remains to be done and as the authors of the DHSS report say it is 'likely that the effect of unemployment on health will be the subject of continuing debate and a fruitful field for further research'.[24]

Consequences For Society In General

There is, then, widespread discussion in the literature about the consequences of unemployment for the young people directly affected. The precise effects are less certain in some areas than others, but the general direction of comment remains. It would be a mistake, however, to suggest that youth unemployment is just, or even primarily a cause for concern because of the consequences it is believed to have for the individuals directly involved. The compassion felt for the young unemployed is important but should not distract attention from the fear that youth unemployment is likely to have serious adverse consequences for society at large.

There are economic consequences of youth unemployment for society in general, just as there are for the individual directly concerned. A recent report by a House of Lords select committee on unemployment[25] reviewed the evidence on the costs of unemployment to the Exchequer. These costs are primarily comprised of first, the loss of revenue from income tax and national insurance contributions and, second, the additional payments that have to be made through national insurance benefits, other social security benefits, rent and rate rebates plus administrative costs. The select committee estimated the total cost to the Exchequer to average £5,000 per person per year. Of course, it is likely that the costs will be lower in the case of younger people: they would

not have contributed so extensively to revenue
because of lower earnings and probably would be
unable to claim a number of benefits available to
older people. Nevertheless, undoubtedly there
would be a cost to the Exchequer. In taking
account of the economic costs of youth unemployment one would also have to consider the loss of
production.

However, just as when considering the consequences of youth unemployment for the individuals directly concerned, so when considering
the consequences for society in general it is
possible to argue that economic considerations
have been less crucial than social ones. Particular concern has been expressed, for example,
about the way that youth unemployment might affect
the capacity to work. One recent study has
argued that:

> there comes a point when people can no
> longer sustain their motivation (to find
> work) in the face of continued rejection,
> heightened awareness of their own short-
> comings, disillusionment with job finding
> services, belief that all available options
> have been covered and a knowledge that jobs
> are scarce anyway. In short, people be-
> come locked into a vicious circle: lack of
> success in job-finding reduces their moti-
> vation and this subsequently reduces even
> further their chances of finding work.[26]

Such problems affect all who are unemployed
but the young are seen to be particularly vulnerable. It is suggested that the years after a
young person leaves school are particularly important in helping to form attitudes and habits that
will affect a person for a lifetime. Gurney[27]
sees them as a critical stage in the psychological
development of young people, arguing that unemployment may hinder such development. Markall
and Gregory, from a somewhat different perspective, talk about these years as 'a critical stage
in the cycle of reproduction of labour power'.
It encompasses, they argue, that transition 'from
the social relations of dependence, which
characterise schooling and the family, to the
heart of the relations of capitalist production
and consumption'. Young people must be prepared
not simply 'for entry into work but, crucially,

for wage labour within the antagonistic social relations of capitalism'.[28] If a young person suffers from a lengthy period of unemployment in these years, or worse still, if they never obtain a job, then they will not develop the habits and discipline that are essential for future working life and it may be impossible to repair the damage. Ridley takes this issue a stage further by suggesting that in some cases unemployment after leaving school may lead to the permanent 'scarring' of the young people concerned.

> Even if the economy did revive, the wasted years could never be offset for the individual by subsequent employment. This is particularly true of the school leaver. Some will never fulfil their work potential because of the absence of opportunities to develop skills in the formative years. Some will be psychologically affected by their apparent rejection by society: though the adult may experience greater financial hardship, it is for the juvenile that the experience is likely to be most traumatic, because he is at the most vulnerable age emotionally. Many will doubtless settle later into formal patterns of work and life, but some will remain permanently scarred.[29]

Of course, such permanent scarring is a cause for concern from the point of view of the individual directly involved: however it is also, and this is the emphasis at this point, a cause for concern for society in general. If a significant proportion of young people are scarred in the manner suggested by Ridley then they may be unable to fit into permanent employment when it becomes available for them in the future. While it has always been accepted that some young people will be unable to fit into normal work patterns it has always been assumed that they will be a small minority. If this small minority were to grow significantly it would pose a threat to the smooth operation of the industrial system and such an occurrence would be seen as a danger in its own right.

One of the most persistent suggestions in the literature about the effects of youth unemployment for society in general has moved away from the issue of ability and willingness to work, to look at the link between youth unemployment and undesirable social behaviour. Particular attention has centred, for example, on the link between youth unemployment and crime and delinquency. There is a large body of literature on this subject, much coming from the U.S.A. but some coming from a range of other countries including Britain. The central conclusion from this writing is the association between crime and youth unemployment. An American researcher, Fleisher, concluded in 1963 that: 'An examination of delinquency rates and other variables by age and through time suggests that the effect of unemployment on juvenile delinquency is positive and significant'.[30] A decade later three other American researchers broadened Fleisher's interest and looked at labour market participation rates rather than just unemployment rates. They noted that during the middle and later 1960s in the U.S.A. crime rates rose while unemployment rates declined. Although at first sight this appears to contradict the link between unemployment and crime, in fact they argued this was not the case because while unemployment rates declined so did participation rates. Thus, they were able to broaden, yet essentially support Fleisher's thesis, concluding 'that labour-market opportunities are sufficient to explain increasing crime rates for youth'.[31] A more recent British study from the Home Office examined the links between unemployment, crime and race in the 1970s.[32] This study, like most previous ones, confirmed the link between arrest rates and unemployment amongst whites but questioned the link amongst other groups. Generally the view has been held that unemployment is more centrally linked to certain kinds of crime, in particular property crimes such as burglary and theft, rather than crime in general.

However, despite the generally accepted association between crime and unemployment rates a number of questions still remain. One of them was recognised by Fleisher in the early study that has already been referred to. He noted in his study that many factors which affect delinquency had not been considered and therefore, one could not assert that unemployment was more important than such factors. This point has been expanded upon in a paper by the National Association for the Care and Resettlement of Offenders:

To observe various instances of correlation
is not, of course, to establish a causal
relationship. It is now generally recognised that many factors are involved in
crime of various kinds and a correlation
between unemployment and crime rates may be
less significant than other correlations,
or that it may be that some other factor is
itself responsible for the observed correlation between unemployment and crime.
Take away the third, or intervening, variable and the correlation disappears. For
instance, an association has also been
found between income and delinquency.
Unemployment is generally accompanied by
poverty. It may be, therefore, that
poverty rather than unemployment is the
determinative factor and this has to be
allowed for. Since the same may also be
true for a whole range of other factors
this can lead to quite complex statistical
processes in an attempt to find out how
important unemployment itself is compared
to other things.[33]

As well as this particular problem there are
others, like for example, the nature of the
figures. Crime figures can be influenced by
factors like reporting rates and improvements in
police efficiency. When juvenile crime is being
considered it is also important to examine the
visibility of certain sections of the population
and the way in which if police attention is concentrated on them the statistics can be distorted.
In both Britain and the U.S.A. there has been
a serious debate over such issues and the interpretation of research results in recent years. In
Britain work by Carr-Hill and Stern[34] has been
used to draw the link between crime and
unemployment into question. In their most recent
study they argued that for the years 1970 to 1981

(i) There is no significant relationship
between increases in recorded crime and
increases in unemployment

(ii) A major part, possibly most, of the
increase in recorded crime may be due to

the increase in the proportion of offences recorded rather than in the number of offences which occur.[35]

They therefore concluded:

This puts increases in crime and their possible relation with increases in unemployment in a very different perspective....It is quite wrong to pretend that there is a well attested relationship. Similarly, it is absurd to lay great emphasis on increases in total serious offences when most of that increase is due to change in the proportion that is recorded. The issues involved are too serious to be treated in the casual way invoked in recent utterances. In particular, given that unemployment is likely to remain high for several years it is grossly unfair on those who may be or become unemployed to associate them with an increase in criminality when the link is not established and the increase itself may be spurious. The case against the high levels of unemployment we are seeing is surely overwhelming for a whole host of reasons. In arguing against these high levels of unemployment, it is therefore both unnecessary and unhelpful to taint the unemployed with criminality.[36]

One recent review of the literature in the U.S.A.[37] reached a similar conclusion. The debate though is far from concluded. Carr-Hill and Stern's work has recently been criticised by Hakim[38] and a recent issue of the Journal of Social Policy carried further comment and a rejoinder.[39] This is clearly an area where despite the body of research evidence that has accumulated over many years there is as yet no clear consensus of interpretation of results.

Apart from the link between undesirable social behaviour and youth unemployment one of the most frequently discussed consequences of youth unemployment is its implications for political attitudes and activity. Many commentators have argued that prolonged high levels of youth unemployment may lead those who have suffered from such conditions to become disenchanted with traditional forms of political activity. Essentially what is argued is that young people may come to believe that the current political system is incapable of dealing with the problems it faces (and in particular the problems that young people themselves face like the lack of employment opportunities) no matter which political party is in power. As a result they will fail to vote in elections or associate themselves with any of the main political parties but instead may turn to more radical solutions: such solutions might mean supporting a more "extreme" party, either of the right or of the left, and/or supporting extra-parliamentary action to achieve desired aims. In this context, in recent years considerable attention has been focussed on the extent of support for the National Front and the associated effect that this might have on race relations.

Fears about the effects of high levels of youth unemployment on the particular social/political attitudes linked to race relations have specific relevance for the unemployed themselves but also have more general relevance. Johoda[40] argues that part of the prevailing climate of opinion, both amongst blacks and whites, is to attribute unemployment to one's race or to the fact that some blacks have jobs while white people are unemployed. She also notes that incidents 'of racial hostility have increased in parallel with the rise in the overall unemployment rate, one of the most frightening examples of the social disintegration that results from the current shrinking of the labour market'.[41] A similar point has been made by Sinfield.[42] He has argued that workers who were happy to see immigrants taking low paid jobs when there was a labour shortage often resent the competition between black and white youths when unemployment is high. He has suggested that in such circumstances the National Front encourages anxieties and fears and boasts of recruitment amongst school leavers, particularly in inner city areas where many of the young unemployed complain that "the blacks" are the cause of unemployment.

A recent issue of Bulldog, the paper of the Young National Front, was headlined "We want jobs not more wages". This was the chant of their march through Nuneaton under the banner 'British jobs for British workers'. Earlier this year it carried a story on social security fraud headlined 'Blackspongers' over another article head-lined 'What about the white workers?' that reported that jobs and housing in different parts of London were being reserved for blacks. In August 1978 Bulldog reported that 'Britain's youth hate the multiracial society that the government is forcing them to live in.' 'They hate being forced to compete for jobs and houses with black for-eigners. They HATE being treated as second class citizens in their own coun-try.' (Quoted a young recruit, 'I didn't think it was right that I couldn't get a job when there were blacks doing jobs I wanted to do. In Britain we should come first.')[43]

In practice, though, as Hakim[44] comments, apart from a very limited amount of opinion poll data on the way in which high levels of unemploy-ment are associated with certain generally held social political views there is very little real information on the political consequences of youth unemployment, particularly the political con-sequences arising from changes in attitude amongst the unemployed themselves. If one looks at the political socialisation literature there is a range of work which shows the way that early influences can shape political attitudes and behaviour (for example, research in the 1950s by Hyman[45] pointed to the crucial role of the family and later work in the U.S.A. and elsewhere argued for attention to be paid to the effect of other influences like the school,[46] work plus a wide range of other social experiences[47]). There is also a debate[48] about the persistence of early socialisation as well as the extent to which significant changes in social position or specific and dramatic events might lead to changes in political attitude and behaviour (in this con-text it is worthwhile noting that research re-ported by Sears and McConahay[49] suggests that the urban riots in the U.S.A. resocialised young blacks). However, there is not such a com-prehensive body of research available directly related to the political consequences of youth un-employment.

Some writers, while accepting that unemployment

has political consequences, have challenged the view that there is any evidence of political extremism as opposed to political apathy on the part of the young unemployed. The following extract, from a study of young unemployed in Merseyside, suggests that there is some evidence of lack of interest in the activities of the traditional political parties and some evidence that dissatisfaction with current circumstances may lead to sporadic outbreaks of social disorder, but less evidence that the activities of the young can be mobilised by political activists.

What we may have among the disadvantaged inner-city young, in other words, is passive alienation. They have opted out of the polity if, indeed, they were ever socialised into it in the first place. There is no sign yet of significant political activity among the young directed against the existing order. Opinions differ about the extent to which alienated youngsters form a pool that could be mobilised by political activists. Conservatives and social democrats may fear it, the far left may hope for it, but I have my doubts. The intellectual demands revolutionary movements make on their members (reading news-sheets, etc) and the commitments of time they demand (selling news sheets, etc) are probably too high. The National Front is another matter, because it offers a rather different outlet for frustrated energies. Street fights are more likely to strike a chord than organised political action. But it is well to remember that riots can be triggered off by all sorts of organisations or, indeed, by no organisations at all. There, perhaps, lies the real danger. A generation idle and frustrated because unemployed; rejected by employers, thus alienated; concentrated in certain districts where the environment itself is grim – not revolution, but simple undirected violence and pointless destruction.[50]

The writer quoted above is not playing down the importance of the political consequences of youth unemployment or suggesting that they should be ignored. Alienation, apathy and disenchantment clearly are not in themselves desirable. What is being questioned is whether such feelings will find expression in organised political activity. What is also being asked is whether the problems now being noted are new, or whether they have existed for many years, and simply have been made worse by the high levels of unemployment. Specifically, were the disadvantaged inner-city young ever really socialised into the polity?

The riots in the summer of 1981 in a number of major British cities led many commentators to see the issue of the link between youth unemployment and urban unrest as being of urgent concern. The precise role of youth unemployment in the events of 1981 is difficult to pin down though it is clear that many of those directly involved in the riots were unemployed and the areas which suffered worst from rioting had recorded particularly high rates of youth unemployment. In practice few doubt that the frustration of the young unemployed and the despair at what the future might hold felt by those still at school provided a fertile background for such social disorder. However, it is questionable whether high rates of unemployment, by themselves, are enough to explain the causes of the riots. After all, by no means all areas with high unemployment suffered serious riots.

The question remains, as well, of the precise links, between even this kind of activity and a challenge to the political system. Were the riots simply another expression of what Ridley referred to as the undirected violence and pointless destruction, and what Stokes[51] has referred to as diffused hostility against the community, or were they an indication of a likely more substantial challenge to social order.

Mungham has little doubt about the answer to this question. He believes that youth unemployment never has provided a real challenge to the social order. He recognises the emergence of racial tensions, their links to riots and disturbances in the late 1970s and the incidents when working class youth have turned their anger and impatience against themselves (for example, in gang disputes) as important. However, he argues that this evidence does not point to a challenge to social order. He suggests that whatever 'threats are posed by elements of contemporary youth are highly specific and partial ones' and 'probably have no wider social significance'.[52] Mungham further suggests that recent attempts to mobilise the young workless have either been ineptly done, or have failed to have a major appeal or have not been attempted at all. He includes in the first category the attempts of young socialists to carve a constituency out of the disaffected young in the 1960s.

> One attempt by the Socialist Labour League to mobilise young people - under the banner of 'Mods and Rockers Must Unite to Kick Out the Tories' - was a typically woeful experiment in politicisation.[53]

The more recent attempt to involve young people in the 'Right to Work Campaign' is included in the second category.

> The campaign's 300 mile march from South Wales (a jobless blackspot) to the Conservative Party Conference at Brighton (a trek which started on 25 September 1980) failed to tap any general support or even to attract much interest nationally. The march ended in Brighton with no more recruits than the 200 who originally set out and most of those were members of the Socialist Workers' Party.[54]

As an example of the third category he points to the failure of the Labour Party and the trade unions to organise unemployed workers of any age. Mungham concludes:

> In historical terms the workless young have never been able to discharge the revolutionary load laid upon them, and there is nothing in the present circumstances to suggest that 'youth' is at last ready to indulge the hopes of political activists or the fears of those who, at a distance, imagine every kind of convulsion and youthful infamy.[55]

Conclusion

The importance of the above discussion is that it shows that youth unemployment can be a cause of concern not simply because of its effects on the young themselves but also because of its consequences for society in general. In this context consequences like the effect of unemployment on 'employability', crime rates and social unrest clearly are important. In practice it has been argued that the evidence on these matters is far from conclusive. For example, the nature and the link between unemployment and crime is still the subject of heated debate. Yet in some ways the precise nature or extent of the link between youth unemployment and these issues may be less important than the fact that such links are widely discussed and believed by many. In the case of policy making the perception of the problem by the policy makers and by those who influence them is more important than anything else.

Before turning to look at these policies, though, we pause for a moment to examine the extent of 'the problem' and some assessments of its causes. This will provide an important background not just for the discussion of policy formation, but also for the evaluation of policy measures. Later, though when the political debate on youth unemployment is reviewed some of the issues raised here will surface again: in particular, issues like the link between unemployment on the one hand, and crime and social unrest on the other.

Notes

1. Department of Health and Social Security cohort study of unemployed men. See B Davies, L Hamill, S Moylan, C H Smee, 'Incomes in and out of work'. Employment Gazette, June 1982, p.237.
2. M Colledge, R Bartholomew, 'The long-term unemployed: some new evidence'. Employment Gazette, January 1980, p.11.
3. Ibid, p.11.
4. A Sinfield, 'Poor and Out-of Work in Shields', in P Townsend (ed) The Concept of Poverty. Heinemann, London, 1971, p.228
5. R E Pahl, 'Family, community and unemployment', New Society, 21 January 1982, pp.91-3.
6. P Eisenberg, P F Lazarfeld, 'The Psychological Effects of Unemployment'. Psychological Bulletin, 1933.

7. A Donovan, M Oddy reported in _Journal of Adolescence_, Vol 5, No.1, p.15.
8. J Miller, _Situation Vacant_, Community Projects Foundation, London, 1982.
9. M H Brenner, 'Mortality and the National Economy: A Review of Experience in England and Wales 1936-76'. _Lancet_, 15 September 1979, pp.568-73.
10. See L Francis, _Youth in Transit_, Gower, Aldershot, 1982.
11. S Platt, study of unemployed men in Edinburgh between 1968 and 1982 reported in _Unemployment Unit Bulletin_, No.10, 1983.
12. R E Pahl, _Op Cit_, p.92.
13. K Roberts _et al_, in _Leisure Studies_, Vol 1, No.2, 1982, p.171.
14. Study reported in _British Journal of Guidance and Counselling_, Vol 10, No.1, 1982.
15. C Brinkmann, 'Finanzielle und psycho-soziale Belastungen wahrend der Arbeitslasigkeit' in A Wacker (ed), _Vom Sckock Zum Fatalismus_, Campus Verlag, Frankfurt, 1981.
16. See M H Banks, C W Clegg, P R Jackson, N J Kemp, E M Stafford, T D Wall, 'The Use of the General Health Questionnaire as an indicator of mental health in occupational studies', _Journal of Occupational Psychology_, 1980, Vol 53, pp.187-94.
17. R E Pahl, _Op Cit_, p.93.
18. See, for example, M J Gardner, _et al_, 'Patterns of mortality in middle and early old age in the county boroughs of England and Wales', _British Journal of Preventative and Social Medicine_, 1969, Vol 23, pp.133-40; M H Brenner, _Op Cit_; M E Brennan, 'Patterns of Mortality and the alienation of life: a study using census indicators' in W H G Armytage, J Peel (eds), _Perimeters of Social Repair_, Academic Press, London, 1978, pp.73-9; M E Brennan, R Lancashire, 'Associations of Childhood mortality with housing status and unemployment', _Journal of Epidemiology and Community Health_, Vol 32, 1978, No 1, pp.28-33.
19. See discussion by S Ramsden, C Smee, 'The health of unemployed men: DHSS cohort study'. _Employment Gazette_, September 1981, pp.397-401.
20. M H Brenner, 1979, _Op Cit_.
21. S Ramsden, C Smee, _Op Cit_.
22. _Ibid_, p.401

23. M Banks, P R Jackson 'Unemployment and the risk of minor psychiatric disorder in young people: cross sectional and longitudinal evidence' in Psychological Medicine, No 12, 1982, pp.789-98.

24. S Ramsden, C Smee, Op Cit, p.401.

25. Report from the Select Committee of the House of Lords on Unemployment, Vol 1, H.M.S.O., London, 1982.

26. M Colledge, R Bartholomew, Op Cit, p.10.

27. M Gurney, 'The effects of unemployment on the psycho-social development of school leavers', Occupational Psychology, 1980, Vol 53, pp.205-13.

28. G Markall, D Gregory, 'Who Cares? The MSC Intervenes: Full of Easter Promise', in T Rees, P Atkinson, Youth Unemployment and State Intervention, Routledge and Kegan Paul, London, 1982, p.59.

29 F F Ridley, 'View from a disaster area: unemployed youth in Merseyside', in B Crick (ed), Unemployment, Methuen, London, 1981, p.27.

30. B M Fleisher, 'The effects of unemployment on juvenile delinquency'. Journal of Political Economy, 1963, Vol 71, p.553.

31. L Phillips, H L Votey, P Maxwell, 'Crime, Youth and the labour market'. Journal of Political Economy, Vol 80, No.3, p.502.

32. P Stevens, C F Willis, Race, Crime and Arrests, Home Office Research Study No.58, H.M.S.O., London, 1979.

33. I Crow, 'The unemployment/crime link', Unemployment Unit Bulletin, 1982, No.4, p.4

34. R A Carr-Hill, N H Stern, Crime, the Police and Criminal Statistics, Academic Press, London, 1979.

35. R A Carr-Hill, N H Stern, 'Crime, unemployment and the police', Research note No.2, SSRC Programme on Taxation, Incentives and the Distribution of Income, International Centre for Economics and Related Disciplines, London School of Economics and Political Science, p.8, quoted in R A Carr-Hill, N H Stern, 'Unemployment and Crime: a Comment', Journal of Social Policy, 1983, Vol 12, Part 3, at p.341.

36. R A Carr-Hill, N H Stern, ibid, pp.8-9, quoted in Journal of Social Policy, article at p.391.

37. C R Little, W J Villemez, D A Smith, 'One step forward, two steps back: more on the class/-criminality controversy', American Sociological Review, June 1982, Vol 47, No.3, pp.435-8.
38. C Hakim, 'The Social Consequences of High Unemployment'. Journal of Social Policy, 1982, Vol 11, Part 4.
39. Journal of Social Policy, 1983, Vol 12, Part 3.
40 Op Cit.
41. Ibid, pp.55-6.
42. A Sinfield, What Unemployment Means, Martin Robertson, Oxford, 1981.
43. Ibid, p.122.
44. Op Cit.
45. H Hyman, Political Socialisation, Free Press, New York, 1959.
46. R E Dowse, J Hughes, 'The Family, the School and the Political Socialisation Process', in R Rose (ed). Studies in British Politics, Macmillan, London, 1976. (3rd edition).
47. D Kavanagh, Political Culture, Macmillan, London, 1972.
48. D O Sears, 'Political Socialisation', in F I Greenstein, N Polsbyn, Micropolitical Theory. Addison Wesley, New York, 1975, pp.93-154.
49. D O Sears, J B McConahay, The Politics of Violence, Houghton-Mifflin, Boston, 1973.
50. F F Ridley, Op Cit, p.26.
51. G Stokes, Unemployment Among School Leavers, University of Birmingham, (mimeo), 1981.
52. G Mungham, 'Workless Youth as a Moral Panic', in T L Rees, P Atkinson, Youth Unemployment and State Intervention, Routledge and Kegan Paul, London 1982, pp.38-9.
53. Ibid, p.37.
54. Ibid, pp.37-8.
55. Ibid, p.39.

Chapter Two

YOUTH UNEMPLOYMENT: THE NATURE OF THE PROBLEM

Recent Trends in Unemployment: the Background to Youth Unemployment

In the thirty years following the second World War Britain enjoyed relatively low rates of unemployment. The rates varied and on occasions rose fairly sharply but such rises were reversed within a year or two. Table 2.1 shows that from 1975 onwards the position changed significantly. Between 1974 and 1975 the unemployment rate rose from 2.7 per cent to 4.1 per cent: more importantly, though, this rise was not reversed in subsequent years. Unemployment rates declined in 1978 and 1979 but only marginally and the upward trend began again in 1980, so that by 1984 almost 13 per cent of the workforce (over 3 million people) was unemployed, about five times what the rate had been in 1974.

Alongside this rise in unemployment rates, another important trend might be noted. Over the same period the average duration of unemployment increased. Table 2.2 shows that whereas in 1974 about 31 per cent of those unemployed had been out of work for six months or more, in 1984 the comparable proportion was 60 per cent. Later it will be noted that many argue that long-term unemployment is a particularly important problem.

Of course, Britain has not been alone in experiencing a rise in the level of unemployment since the mid 1970s. Most Western nations have faced similar problems. Table 2.3 shows that the rise in unemployment rates in Britain has been matched fairly closely in a number of other countries (the best example is Belgium): some other countries have not suffered as much as Britain,

Table 2.1:   Unemployment Rate, U.K. 1960-1984

Year	Percentage Unemployed*
1960	1.7
1961	1.6
1962	2.1
1963	2.6
1964	1.5
1965	1.6
1966	2.5
1967	2.5
1968	2.5
1969	2.5
1970	2.6
1971	3.3
1972	3.7
1973	2.6
1974	2.6
1975	4.0
1976	5.5
1977	5.8
1978	5.7
1979	5.4
1980	6.9
1981	10.4
1982	12.1
1983	12.9
1984+	12.8

* Numbers registered unemployed as a percentage of estimated total number of employees.

+ Figure for May 1984

Note - Figures from 1971 onwards calculated on new basis, described in Employment Gazette, December 1982, p.S20.

Annual Abstract of Statistics, 1972, p.143,
Employment Gazette, December 1982, S22, June 1984, S24.

Table 2.2: Unemployment by Duration, G.B. 1974–1984

Year	2 weeks or less %	2-4 weeks %	4-8 weeks %	8-13 weeks %	13-26 weeks %	26-52 weeks %	Over 52 weeks %
1974	20.8	12.1	11.3	10.3	14.3	10.9	20.2
1975	15.3	15.4	14.4	11.8	16.1	12.3	14.7
1976	9.8	7.4	12.4	12.3	20.3	20.9	17.1
1977	9.5	7.2	11.4	11.4	18.7	19.7	22.2
1978	7.9	6.9	10.3	10.2	17.8	19.9	27.0
1979	6.2	6.2	10.2	10.6	17.8	18.8	30.2
1980	8.6	7.1	12.0	12.0	18.7	18.3	23.3
1981	6.2	5.4	9.9	11.4	22.1	24.6	20.4
1982	4.3	4.6	8.0	8.7	17.4	23.9	33.1
1983	5.8	4.4	7.1	7.7	16.2	22.7	36.1
1984	5.0	3.7	6.7	8.0	15.6	21.7	39.2

Notes: 1. Percentages refer to total number of people unemployed at April of that year.
2. Figures for 1980–84 cover UK.

Source: Department of Employment Gazette 1977, October, p.1159, Employment Gazette 1980, October, p.S33, Employment Gazette 1982, October, p.S34, June 1984, S38

Table 2.3: Standardised Unemployment Rates – International Comparisons 1970–82

Per cent of total labour force

	1970	1971	1972	1973	1974	1975	1976	1977	1978	1979	1980	1981	1982
Australia	1.6	1.9	2.6	2.3	2.6	4.8	4.7	5.6	6.2*	6.2	6.0	5.7	7.1
Austria	1.4	1.3	1.2	1.1	1.4	1.7	1.8	1.6	2.1	2.1	1.9	2.5	3.5
Belgium	2.1	2.2	2.7	2.8	3.1	5.1	6.6	7.5	8.1	8.4	9.0	11.1	13.0*
Canada	5.6	6.1	6.2	5.5	5.3	6.9	7.1	8.0	8.3	7.4	7.5	7.5	10.9
Finland	1.9	2.2	2.5	2.3	1.7	2.2	4.0	6.0	7.4	6.0	4.8	5.2	6.1
France	2.4	2.6	2.7	2.6	2.8	4.1	4.4	4.7	5.2	5.9	6.3	7.3	8.0*
Germany	0.8*	0.9*	0.8*	0.8*	1.6*	3.6*	3.7*	3.6*	3.5*	3.2*	3.0*	4.4*	6.1
Italy	5.3	5.3	6.3	6.2	5.3	5.8	6.6	7.0	7.1	7.5	7.4	8.3	8.9
Japan	1.1	1.2	1.4	1.3	1.4	1.9	2.0	2.0	2.2	2.1	2.0	2.2	2.4
Netherlands	1.0*	1.3*	2.2*	2.2*	2.7*	3.9*	4.2*	4.1	4.1	4.1	4.7	7.0	9.6*
Norway	1.6*	1.5*	1.7	1.5	1.5	2.3	1.8	1.5	1.8	2.0	1.7	2.0	2.6
Spain	2.4*	3.1*	3.1*	2.5*	2.6*	3.7*	4.7*	5.2*	6.9*	8.5	11.2	14.0	15.9
Sweden	1.5	2.5	2.7	2.5	2.0	1.6	1.6	1.8	2.2	2.1	2.0	2.5	3.1
United States	4.8	5.8	5.5	4.8	5.5	8.3	7.5	6.9	5.9	5.7	7.0	7.5	9.5
United Kingdom	3.1*	3.9*	4.2*	3.2*	3.2	4.7	6.0*	6.3*	6.3*	5.6*	7.0*	10.7*	12.5*

Note: Data have been adjusted (as far as possible) both to preserve comparability over time and to conform with the definitions drawn up by the International Labour Organisation. The adjustments mainly affect countries that base their unemployment statistics on registration records maintained by employment offices. Where necessary the OECD has tried to adjust "registered" unemployment with a view to including unemployed persons not covered on the register and to excluding employed persons still carried on the register. For several countries the adjustment procedure used is similar to that of the U.S. Department of Labor. Minor differences may appear mainly because the rates published by the U.S. Department of Labor refer to the civilian labour force. Series adjusted by the OECD are marked by an asterisk (*).

Source: OECD Economic Outlook, July 1983, No.33, p.169

though even those have not escaped entirely
(unemployment rates in Japan, for example, are
still very low by comparison though they have also
risen significantly since 1974).

It is worthwhile stressing, at this juncture,
that caution needs to be exercised in interpreting
unemployment figures. This warning applies even
if only the unemployment figures of one country
are being looked at. For example, in Britain
traditionally the unemployment figures have
covered only those who have registered as such.
However, many people fail to register as unemployed, especially if they are unable to claim
financial assistance from the state. This means
that many young people, and women in particular,
fail to register. A recent study of non-
registration amongst young people[1] showed widely
varying percentages of non-registration from one
area to another (the highest percentage recorded
was where young people who were unemployed were
not registered as such, on average, for 48 per
cent of the time). Overall, non-registration
accounted for 22 per cent of the time that the
young people were unemployed. A further consideration, in Britain, is that the figures do not
cover those who are supported by Government
special employment measures. This has been the
cause of some debate: the Government has argued
that it is right that these people should not be
counted for they are not unemployed and seeking
work, but critics would reply that if a measure is
desired of the extent to which normal job opportunities cannot be found by those who want them
then such people need to be counted in the
total. The position in Britain has been further
complicated by changes made to practice since
1982. Since October 1982 the unemployment
figures have been based on those claiming benefit
rather than on those registered as unemployed and
available for work. Further changes made in
April 1983 mean that most long-term unemployed
people aged 60 and over are now also removed from
the official figures. The effect of these
changes can be seen by noting that in June 1984
the total number unemployed on the new basis of
counting was 3,036,200 (including school leavers)
whereas on the pre November 1982 basis of counting
the figure would have been 3,547,800. If one
also wanted to make an allowance for the other
factors, like non-registration, which were not

taken in account on the 'old' basis of compiling the unemployment figures, then one might add to this figure: those who do not register as unemployed but are still seeking work (estimates of this number vary from between 400,000 to over 600,000), those who have dropped out of the labour market, and therefore currently are not seeking jobs, but who would do so if they thought that jobs were available (economic activity rates rose throughout most of the 1970s but declined towards the end - if one assumed that they would not have declined had jobs been available and might have kept on rising, then the additional figure to be counted might be anything from three quarters of a million to a million), and those currently covered by special employment measures (up to 500,000). The figures indicate that an unemployment figure for June 1984 of around 5 million could be claimed, or over 20 per cent, given certain assumptions about the labour market and the behaviour of the unemployed[2].

There is a view that some of these calculations need to be balanced by an allowance for the number of people who are claiming unemployment and supplementary benefit but who are not really seeking work. This would include people who it is said prefer to 'live off' unemployment or supplementary benefit rather than work. Similarly allowance needs to be made for those people who are looking for work but who will not accept 'low wage' jobs. There is a view, for instance, that there are many low wage jobs available particularly in the service sector, but the unemployed will not accept them. In this way it is argued that a great deal of unemployment is really voluntary. Again, allowance also needs to be made for those people working in 'the black economy'. Assessment of these factors is even more difficult than is the case with those issues raised in the last paragraph and is even more controversial. For example, it is arguable that many people working in 'the black economy' may already have jobs and therefore may not be counted in the unemployment figures. There is reason to believe that as the recession has deepened the proportion of those working in 'the black economy' who have another job will have increased because they are those who have shown by their success in the labour market that they have skills in demand. It is not necessary, though, to try to resolve the debate here for the essential point is simply that the unemployment figures need to be interpreted cautiously for they clearly do not offer a complete guide to the problem.

The problems faced when interpreting the unemployment figures of one country, are multiplied when international comparisons are made. For example, despite the adoption of ILO guidelines in 1954 the collection of the figures by individual countries varies tremendously. In some countries (like Australia, Canada, Japan, Italy, Sweden and the U.S.A.) unemployment figures are based on labour force sample surveys whereas in others (like France, Germany and Britain) they are based on monthly counts at unemployment offices or on insurance statistics. There are also major differences in the definitions used. In some countries people are only counted as being unemployed if they are out of work for a whole week, whereas in others unemployment is simply measured on particular days. Similarly countries adopt different minimum age criteria for defining the unemployed, and the basis of the labour force definitions used for computing the crude unemployment figures to percentages varies. A number of attempts have been made to deal with such problems: for instance, by the United States Bureau of Labor Statistics and by the OECD. These attempts have taken the form of adjusting the national figures using common definitions. In some cases they make relatively little difference to the unemployment rate, though in others the difference is more marked (in the case of Italy they mean that if the United States Bureau of Labor Statistics figures are used instead of the national figures, the unemployment percentages for 1977, 1978 and 1979 are reduced from 6.5, 7.1 and 7.6 per cent to 3.4, 3.7 and 4.3 per cent respectively)[3].

Apart from the problem of definition of terms other issues need to be examined in the case of international as well as simple national comparisons. Many countries use special measures which have the effect of taking people off the unemployment register: the problem is that they all use different measures, and the extent to which they are used varies. Maddison suggests that such measures have been used particularly extensively in West Germany[4]. For example, the West German government has managed to keep the unemployment

figures lower than they would have been otherwise
by restrictions on migration (in the five years
1973-78 the foreign labour force in West Germany
fell by 555,000 whereas in the previous five years
it had risen by one and a half million), by
encouraging people to withdraw from the labour
force (it has been estimated that the schemes
designed to encourage early retirement or retrain-
ing took 642,000 out of the labour force in 1978)
and by encouraging work sharing. There is some
evidence that in recent years it has been more
difficult to deal with high unemployment by
restrictions on labour migration. Many foreign
workers have remained in the host country because
of the fear that restrictive immigration policies
would make it impossible for them to return if
they left. Nevertheless, in the past this has
been an important factor influencing reported
unemployment rates. In Japan the measures used
have differed from those of West Germany, but have
had a similarly significant effect on the unemployment figures. In Japan the unemployment
figures are lower than they might have been otherwise because of the tradition amongst Japanese
firms of recruiting people for the whole of their
working life and looking after them for all of
this period (and sometimes beyond into retirment),
to the extent that they may be retained even when
there is no work for them to do. In Sweden the
"active labour market" policies are highly developed. Sorrentino[5] points out that between 1973
and 1977 Sweden spent over 2 per cent of its GNP
on labour market measures: in Britain, U.S.A.,
Canada, Australia and France the comparable figure
was around 0.5 per cent or less. The Swedish
labour market policies have had a major impact on
the level of recorded unemployment: for example,
without them the unemployment rate in 1978 might
have been 6.2 per cent rather than 2.2 per cent.
    These comments are meant simply as a note of
caution. Really there is little alternative
other than to use the official unemployment
figures if one wants to discuss trends or make
comparisons. It is important, though, to be
aware of the basis of the calculation of the
figures, and to be aware that when international
comparisons are being made, in particular, differences in the basis of calculation can have a major
impact. It is also arguable, despite the counter
claims reported earlier, that in virtually all

Youth Unemployment: The Nature of the Problem

cases, the unemployment figures underestimate rather than overestimate the extent of the problem.

Recent Trends in Youth Unemployment

In many ways the trends in youth unemployment mirror those for overall unemployment. As in the case of overall unemployment variations occurred in the youth unemployment rate for the period from the end of the Second World War to the mid 1970s but any rises were fairly quickly reversed, and there was no general prolonged trend for rates to rise (the exact position in the mid 1970s is difficult to determine because figures are not available for 1973, 1974 and 1975, though there is reason to believe that the rate decreased a little after 1972). However, as can be seen from Table 2.4, in the mid 1970s the position changed. Unemployment rates began to increase fairly steadily, and although there were marginal reductions in the rates in 1979, by 1984 the rate was almost three times what it had been in 1976.

Similarly from the mid 1970s onwards the average duration of unemployment amongst young people also lengthened, much as it did amongst the unemployed in general. Thus, table 2.5 shows that whereas in 1975 about 18 percent of all unemployed aged less than 25 had been out of work for over 6 months, the comparable proportion in 1984 was 46 percent (the table refers to the under 25 age range rather than to the under 20s because comparisons over time from official figures are easier to make on this basis: it might also be noted that some international agencies define youth unemployment by using an age under 25 cut off point).

The general similarity in the movement of overall and youth unemployment rates in recent years, though, should not be allowed to obscure a number of important differences. First, youth unemployment rates have been higher than overall unemployment rates throughout the period under consideration. Generally, unemployment rates have decreased with age, except for the oldest age ranges. Second, youth unemployment rates have increased more quickly than overall unemployment rates in recent years, even though both rates have been moving in the same direction. Third, though the duration rates for youth unemployment have increased since the mid 1970s, generally young

Youth Unemployment: The Nature of the Problem

Table 2.4:   Youth Unemployment, Great Britain,
             1965-1984

	% Under 18	% 18-19
1965	1.5	1.6
1966	1.3	1.5
1967	2.3	2.9
1968	2.3	3.2
1969	2.1	3.0
1970	2.5	3.4
1971	3.2	4.3
1972	5.4	6.8
1973		
1974		
1975		
1976	8.5	9.5
1977	13.5	10.3
1978	14.5	10.9
1979	11.8	10.4
1980	11.0	10.5
1981	19.2	17.2
1982	22.6	22.9
1983	24.2	25.8
1984	23.0	27.2

Notes:

1. All percentage rates are estimates. The rates
   between 1965 and 1972 are based on the total
   number of employees in the relevant age group
   and the number registered as unemployed. The
   basis of the calculation for the rate from 1976
   is given in the Employment Gazette, July 1977,
   pp.718-19.
2. All rates refer to January of the year
   concerned. Rates fluctuate considerably
   throughout the year and on occasions have been
   very much higher in July than in January
   because of the number of school leavers unable
   to find employment.
3. Rates for 1983 and 1984 refer to the U.K.

Sources:

(a) Up to 1972
    Annual Abstract of Statistics, relevant years
    British Labour Statistics, relevant years
(b) 1976 and after
    Employment Gazette, December 1979, p.1258
    Employment Gazette, October 1982, p.S37
    Employment Gazette, June 1984, p.S40

Youth Unemployment: The Nature of the Problem

Table 2.5:   Duration of Unemployment for Those
             Aged Under 25, 1976-1984

	Up to 26 weeks	Over 26 weeks Up to 52 weeks	Over 52 weeks
	%	%	%
1976	81.5	13.6	4.9
1977	72.4	17.9	9.7
1978	70.2	19.0	10.8
1979	71.8	17.4	10.8
1980	74.2	15.5	10.2
1981	68.6	21.6	9.8
1982	57.4	22.2	20.4
1983	56.4	20.3	23.3
1984	53.6	18.9	27.5

Note 1:   1.   Figures refer to GB from 1976-80 and
               U.K. from 1981-4.
          2.   Figures refer to January each year.

Sources:
Department of Employment Gazette, 1976, p.129
Department of Employment Gazette, 1977, p.136
Employment Gazette, October 1982, p.532
Employment Gazette, June 1984, p.534

people who have been unemployed have been out of work for a shorter period than older workers. Thus in 1975 less than 5 per cent of young people (under 25) unemployed had been out of work for more than one year whereas the comparable figure for the unemployed in general was almost 15 per cent. It should be noted, though, that by 1984 the difference between the figures had narrowed considerably. In that year over 27 per cent of young people had been unemployed for more than a year while the proportion for the unemployed in general was about 39 per cent. Thus, whereas in 1975 the ratio between under 25 and all ages was 1:3, in 1984 it was about 1:1.5.

When trends in overall unemployment were being considered it was noted that the British experience, whilst different in detail from that of other countries, showed many general similarities. The same comment can be made about youth unemployment. Table 2.6 shows the youth unemployment rate in a number of different countries between 1960 and 1982. In all of the countries listed the youth unemployment rate in 1982 was higher than it had been in 1973 and in most cases substantially higher. For example, in West Germany the rate increased ninefold between 1973 and 1984 while in France and Italy it increased about threefold (rather more than in Italy). In the U.S.A. and Canada the youth unemployment rate increased by a smaller proportion though it should be noted that in both of these countries the youth unemployment rate was very high by comparison at the start of the period. Nevertheless, it is worthwhile commenting that the increase in the youth unemployment rate was greater in Britain than in any of the other countries listed apart from West Germany (the figures are different from those shown in Table 2.4 because they refer to those under 25 years of age).

The Problems of Particular Groups

Youth unemployment, as one might imagine, has not affected all sections of society equally. The general figures and trends hide important variations between groups and sections of society. As a starting point comment might be made about differences related to age and sex. Table 2.7 offers a more detailed analysis of the information presented in Table 2.5. From

Table 2.6: Youth Unemployment Rates 1960-1982, International Comparisons

	1960	1970	1973	1976	1977	1978	1979	1980	1981	1982
United States	10.0	9.9	9.8	14.0	13.0	11.7	11.3	13.3	14.3	17.0
Japan	1.4	2.0	2.2	3.1	3.5	3.8	3.4	3.6	4.0	4.4
West Germany	0.7[a]	0.4	1.0	5.2	5.4	4.8	3.4	3.9	6.5	9.5
France	4.2[b]	5.6	6.3	10.1	11.1	11.0	13.3	15.0	17.0	20.3
U.K.	-	2.9	2.8	12.5	14.3	13.5	11.6	15.3	19.5	21.6
Italy	3.1	9.7	11.9	13.9	22.9	23.9	25.6	25.2	27.4	29.7
Canada	10.7	9.9	9.5	12.6	14.3	14.3	13.0	13.2	13.3	18.7

Youth Unemployment rate defined as unemployment aged 15-24 as a percentage of total labour force aged 15-24.

a. Rate for 1958
b. Rate for 1962

Source: OECD Economic Outlook, Vol 27 (July 1980) p.23, Vol.34 (December 1983), p.46

Table 2.7:   Unemployment by Sex and Age,
             Great Britain, 1965-1984

	% Under 18		% 18-19	
	Male	Female	Male	Female
1965	1.8	1.2	1.9	1.3
1966	1.6	1.0	1.8	1.1
1967	2.8	1.8	3.9	2.0
1968	2.9	1.7	4.4	2.0
1969	2.7	1.5	4.4	1.7
1970	3.3	1.7	5.0	1.9
1971	4.1	2.4	5.9	2.5
1972	4.6	4.2	9.2	4.3
1973				
1974				
1975				
1976	12.3	12.0	11.2	8.1
1977	12.8	14.1	11.1	9.9
1978	13.2	11.2	15.5	11.1
1979	10.8	10.7	12.0	10.3
1980	10.3	11.9	10.7	10.3
1981	19.1	19.2	18.4	15.8
1982	23.1	22.0	25.2	20.2
1983	25.7	29.2	22.1	22.2
1984	24.8	30.3	21.0	23.8

Notes:
All percentage rates are estimates as for table 2.4

Sources:
(a)   Up to 1972
      Annual Abstract of Statistics, relevant years
      British Labour Statistics, relevant years

(b)   1976 and after
      Employment Gazette, December 1979, p.1258
      Employment Gazette, October 1982, p.S34
      Employment Gazette, June 1984, p.S40

table 2.7 it can be seen that the relative positions of under 18s and 18-19 year olds have changed on a number of occasions, even in the short period considered in the table. Generally the under 18s experienced lower rates of unemployment than the 18 and 19 year olds prior to 1976, but higher ones afterwards. This was not the case, though, in 1978, 1979, 1980 and 1982 for males. In 1979 and 1980 youth unemployment rates were falling and the under 18s appear to have gained particular benefit from the improvement in the general position. It is also worth noting that to a large extent the relatively high unemployment percentage recorded for the under 18s during periods of rising unemployment has been a reflection of the dominance of school leavers in this age group. Table 2.8 shows the percentage of school leavers unemployed between 1974/75 and 1981/82. From this table it can be seen that in this period school leaver unemployment has been higher than the overall figure for the under 18s. It can also be seen that school leaver unemployment declined markedly in 1978/79 and 1979/80 although it rose again just as dramatically in the following year.

The differences in unemployment rates between the sexes are marked, but like the differences between age ranges, have changed on a number of occasions over the period examined. It may be worthwhile noting before the specific instance of youth unemployment is looked at that generally male unemployment rates have been higher than female unemployment rates. When youth unemployment is examined the rate for 18 and 19 year olds generally has mirrored the overall trend but the relative position for under 18s has not been quite as consistent. Explanations cannot be examined in any detail at this stage but two points might be made. First, the figures for female unemployment are affected not just by the issue of non-registration but also by withdrawal from the labour market, and withdrawal from the labour market is likely to increase with age for females. Second, female employment is concentrated in certain industries and occupations and therefore female unemployment will be affected by the state of the labour market in particular industries as well as by the more general position.

A considerable amount of attention has been paid in recent years to the imbalance in economic

Table 2.8: School Leavers Unemployed, England and Wales 1974/75-1981/82

	% unemployed
1974/75	8.7
1975/76	18.0
1976/77	20.3
1977/78	24.1
1978/79	12.7
1979/80	12.2
1980/81	24.7
1981/82	26.5

Note: Unemployment in the academic year following attainment of the statutory school leaving age based on the January count suitably adjusted.

Source: Social Trends, Vol.14, 1984, p.46

activity between the regions. Attempts have been made, through a variety of policy measures, to attract industry to areas that have suffered from higher than average levels of unemployment. However, despite attempts, considerable differences remain. In 1981, for example, the unemployment rate in the Northern region was over 15 per cent while in the South East it was about 18 per cent. If one looked below the regional level then even greater differences would be uncovered. Recent studies[6] have suggested that the recession of the late 1970s and early 1980s has led to an increase in the traditional disparities between the regions.

The differences in the labour market between the regions as one would expect are reflected in youth unemployment rates. There are major differences in rates between one part of the country and another. A report from the National Employment Council argued that the area in which a person lives often is the most important determinant of whether or not they get a job: more important than other factors, like skill or training[7]. However, it is important to note that while major differences can be seen between the youth unemployment rates in different parts of the country frequently these differences are less marked than those amongst adult workers. This might be illustrated by referring to a comparison between two particular counties in England, one which has had a relatively high and the other which has had a relatively low unemployment rate: the two counties are Cleveland and Surrey. The 1981 census showed that the overall unemployment rate in Cleveland was 15.5 per cent and in Surrey 3.4 per cent: the unemployment rate for the under 18s at the same time was 25.2 per cent in Cleveland and 10.9 per cent in Surrey and the rate for the 18 and 19 year olds was 26.5 per cent in Cleveland and 8.2 per cent in Surrey[8]. Thus, if the two counties are compared the overall unemployment rate in Cleveland was over four and a half times that in Surrey, but the rate for the under 18s in Cleveland was less than two and a half times that in Surrey and the rate for the 18 and 19 year olds in Cleveland was less than three and a half times that in Surrey.

One possible explanation for this position may be that in areas where unemployment generally is high young people may decide to remain in full-time education longer than they would have done otherwise[9]. There is some evidence which is not directly related to the issue under discussion but which nevertheless supports this view. As unemployment generally has risen in recent years, so the proportion of young people staying on at school and entering non-advanced education has risen. In 1974/75 26.1 per cent of all young people stayed at school in the year following their attainment of the statutory school leaving age and a further 11.5 per cent entered non-advanced further education: by 1981/82 30.5 per cent were staying on at school and a further 16.2 per cent were entering non-advanced further education[10].

The published unemployment figures do not enable one to comment directly on the extent to which youth unemployment affects particular social groups or individuals with particular educational backgrounds or qualifications worse than others. However, a number of specially commissioned surveys enable some comment to be made. For example, a survey carried out for the Manpower Services Commission in 1977[11] showed that many unemployed young people came from social backgrounds that were likely to increase the problems they faced:

> Most (93%) were living at home in what are quite large family units (the mean household size was 5.3 persons). There was a considerable amount of unemployment amongst other family members: 14% had fathers who were unemployed (this increased to 21% in Glasgow), 22% at least one unemployed brother or sister and 19% lived in households where no-one was in full-time work....

> One in four (26%) of the young people in the Unemployed Survey said most or all of their friends were unemployed and nearly four in five (79%) had some friends unemployed; this reflects the concentration of unemployment in areas and among social groups[12].

The same survey showed that the young unemployed generally seemed to have no or lower level school qualifications than other young people.

The unemployed young people were generally less successful at school. They were much more likely to have few or no qualifications than were either the young people in employment or those in full-time education. Just over half (53%) of those in the Unemployed Survey had no qualifications; 28% had only CSEs less than grade 1 and only 19% had one or more GCE 'O' level or CSE grade 1. The boys were more likely to have no qualifications than the girls: 60% of the boys in the Unemployed Survey had no qualification compared with 46% of the girls[13].

It is also worthwhile noting that in this survey it was found that qualifications related to duration as well as likely incidence of unemployment; those young people with the lowest level or no qualifications were more likely than others to experience unemployment lasting for more than six months.

Apart from general social and education factors one of the other variables that has been shown to be linked to unemployment is ethnic grouping. Research has shown that generally certain ethnic groups, though not all, suffer from above average unemployment rates[14]. This general position is mirrored in the particular case of youth unemployment. For example, an analysis of the 1981 Labour Force Survey[15] shows that in the age group 16-24 non-whites suffer much more from unemployment than whites. The rate of unemployment amongst males for West Indians and Guyanese in this age group was almost twice as high as it was for whites; amongst females the unemployment rate for Indians, Pakistanis and Bangladeschi's again was about twice as high as it was for whites. Similar findings have been produced by more detailed studies of unemployment experience in particular localities. Dex, in a study of unemployment in Bradford and Sheffield[16] noted that West Indian and Asian school leavers took much longer to find a job than others after they left school. She also found that the number of times Asian and West Indians were unemployed for a month or more after starting employment was considerably higher for blacks than whites. The reason for this was not that West Indian and Asian youths were any more likely to lose their jobs than white youths, but that once unemployed they had a higher probability of remaining out of work. She argued that this was the result of discrimination against black youths as they applied for jobs. Dex also suggested that members of ethnic minority groups are more likely to drop out of the labour market when unemployed than white youths. In doing so she was supporting the findings of other research in this area. Of course, if members of ethnic minority groups drop out of the labour market they will not be counted in the official unemployment figures.

Another study of ethnic minority groups in one of the same towns surveyed by Dex, Bradford, tried to discover why Asian school leavers suffered particularly badly in the employment market[17]. Campbell and Jones found that only 28 per cent of Asian youths obtained employment after leaving school (41 per cent were unemployed and 31 per cent on special employment schemes) as compared to 66 per cent of all Bradford school leavers (20 per cent of all school leavers were unemployed and 14 per cent on special employment schemes). They argued that the differences in employment experience could not be put down to differences in the level of qualifications (the Asian school leavers, they argued, were at least as well if not better qualified than white school leavers), or to cultural/language problems (two thirds of Asian school leavers had been born in the UK or had received all of their education here). According to Campbell and Jones, the real reason for the employment experience of Asian school leavers was racial discrimination. The discrimination, they suggested, arises because of the ascription of certain characteristics to Asians by employers. 'This discrimination may not be conscious but rather based on stereotyping of young Asians' abilities/skills, their skin colour being associated with certain characteristics and the notion that young Asians, even those born and educated in Bradford, are "fit" for only certain kinds of work - work that is increasingly scarce due to changes in industrial structure and, especially, the labour process.'[18]

The way in which youth unemployment has affected particular groups could be discussed further but probably enough has been said for the moment to enable the essential arguments to be displayed. The central point to be made is that youth unemployment does not affect all sectors of society equally but affects certain sections more than others. Generally the people worst affected by youth unemployment are those that social scientists have long argued suffer most in other problem areas. This means that youth unemployment is only part of a more general picture of disadvantage.

Conclusion

The rise in the level of youth unemployment since the mid 1970s has been dramatic and sustained. In many parts of the country a majority of school leavers are unable to find work. While there is debate on the accuracy and the interpretation of the unemployment figures few would deny that the problem has grown significantly since the mid 1970s. Similarly all the evidence suggests that the position may not improve markedly, at least for the medium term future

The rise in the level of unemployment means that no major section of society has entirely escaped from its effects. However, it has been shown that certain sections of society have suffered more than others and that these sections are the ones that already face serious disadvantage. The reinforcement of this disadvantage is important: it may mean, for example, that many of the young unemployed will be members of families where others are unemployed and therefore as was argued in Chapter 1 will be less likely to be able to look for financial support from that direction.

There have been many similarities between the general trends of unemployment overall and the pattern of youth unemployment. However, youth unemployment does not simply follow overall patterns and in certain areas there are important variations which establish youth unemployment as a topic worthy of consideration in its own right. In particular it appears that youth unemployment seems to rise more swiftly than overall unemployment during the early stages of a depression.

In the next chapter the causes of youth unemployment will be examined. The differences between the trends of youth and overall unemployment mean that one cannot simply rely on general explanations for the particular case of youth unemployment. Nevertheless, this still leaves open the question of whether youth unemployment is a reaction to general economic factors (which might affect youth and adult unemployment in different ways) or whether it is a reaction to problems peculiar to young people.

Notes

1. K Roberts, J Duggan, M Noble, 'Ignoring the Sign: Young, Unemployed and Unregistered', Employment Gazette, August 1981, pp.353-6.
2. For a discussion of the interpretation of unemployment figures see Unemployment Unit Briefing, No.5, November 1982. This discussion refers to November 1982 but outlines the basis of some of the calculations.
3. See Employment Gazette, August 1980, pp.833-40.
4. A Maddison, 'Measuring Labour-Slack', Employment Gazette, July 1980, pp.727-33.
5. C Sorrentino, 'Unemployment in International Perspective', in B Showler, A Sinfield, The Workless State, Martin Robertson, Oxford, 1981.
6. See Cambridge Economics Policy Review, 1982, for a discussion.
7. National Youth Employment Council, Unquali- fied, Untrained and Unemployed, HMSO London, 1974.
8. 1981 Census figures. Census unemployment figures are higher than those quoted by the Department of Employment because they are not restricted to those registed as unemployed, or claiming benefit.
9. See P Makeham, Youth Unemployment, Department of Employment Research Paper No.10 HMSO London, 1980.
10. Social Trends, Vol.4, 1984, p.46.
11. Survey undertaken by Social and Community Research Planning in 1977 for the Manpower Services Commission.
12. Quoted in Manpower Services Commission, Young People and Work, Manpower Studies No.19781, HMSO London, 1978, pp.12-13.
13. Ibid, pp.13-14.
14. D J Smith, 'Unemployment and Racial Minority Groups', Employment Gazette, June 1980, pp.602-6, summarises a fuller report published by P.E.P. later that year.
15. See Employment Gazette, June 1984, 'Unemploy- ment and Ethnic Origin', pp.260-4 for details.

16. S Dex, 'A Note on Discrimination in Employment and its Effects on Black Youths', Journal of Social Policy, Vol.8, No.3, pp.357-69.
17. M Campbell, D Jones,'Racial Discrimination against Asian School Leavers', Unemployment Unit Bulletin, No.5, October 1982, pp.4-5.
18. Ibid, p.5.

Chapter Three

THE CAUSES OF YOUTH UNEMPLOYMENT

In the conclusion to the last chapter it was noted
that one of the questions still to be looked at
was the extent to which explanations of youth
unemployment should be based centrally on factors
specific to the young themselves or whether youth
unemployment should be seen much more as a reflection of general economic problems. This is one
of the central issues to be examined in this
chapter.

In fact, there is a long list of writing and
comment that can be pointed to in support of both
of these broad propositions. For example, a
number of influential political figures, as well
as researchers have suggested that the level of
youth unemployment is not simply a reflection of
general economic conditions but it is also a
reflection of more particular factors: for
instance, the character and attitude of the young
themselves, demographic and related changes,
variations in the relative wage costs of younger
and older workers, and structural changes in
industry. Others though, have challenged such
claims and have argued that youth unemployment is
much more a reflection of general economic conditions than a result of factors specifically
related to the positions of the young. Such an
argument, of course, begs the question about what
determines general economic conditions and overall
unemployment rates. However, such an argument
clearly locates the discussion of youth unemployment as part of this more general debate rather
than as something special and separate from it.

It is intended to look, first of all, at the
argument that youth unemployment is primarily the
result of specific factors reflecting the position

and abilities of the young and then at the argument that it can better be accounted for by
general economic conditions. In each case the
basis of the argument will be summarised and the
kind of evidence available pointed to. After
this review an attempt will be made to assess the
relative strengths of these arguments as explanations, either on their own or in combination.
An assessment of their value in combination
clearly is important for many of these factors
would not be expected to operate in isolation.

The Character and Attitudes of the Young

One of the claims most frequently made about the
young, which is used as an explanation for the
level of unemployment amongst that age group, is
that they are no longer attractive recruits for
employers. The claim contains a number of inter-
related elements. First, it is argued that the
young do not have the 'right attitude to work':
this is usually taken to mean that they do not
accept work discipline, that their time-keeping is
bad, and that they show little enthusiasm for the
work itself. Second, it is argued that often the
young do not possess the necessary educational
qualities: in particular that they lack the most
basic skills. Third, it is suggested that their
personal appearance is unacceptable: employers
dislike the clothes they wear and they are accused
of not taking sufficient 'care' over their appearance. Such comments imply a comparison both with
older workers, and with previous generations.
    There is some evidence that a number of
employers hold such views and that it might
influence their recruitment policies (of course,
such evidence does not mean that employers are
correct in their assessment but even if they are
not correct such views may be important for they
may influence hiring policy). Thus, one large
scale survey of employers from all sections of
industry, except central Government, found that a
large proportion (though not a majority) of
employers surveyed believed that young people
displayed a poorer 'attitude to work' than older
workers: more importantly, about three quarters
of all respondents to this survey stated that a
'good attitude to work' was essential for all
recruits. A number of "typical" remarks were
quoted to show the kind of things employers were

saying and the kind of reasons they were giving for not employing young people.

Lack of enthusiasm: one detects a certain feeling that they are only half wanting the job. One also feels that with low retail wages they would prefer to be on the dole.

The most common one is general appearance and attitude during the interview. I have them coming in with dirty fingernails, untidy hair, tatty dress, which shows what their general attitude to work would be.

Poor educational standards, unable to fill in a test form. Poor general appearance[1].

A claim frequently made is that the problems referred to above are in large measure a reflection of faults in the educational system. Schools no longer teach the 'basic skills' and the educational system does not prepare young people adequately for the world of work. The courses in the last few years at school are seen as irrelevant by many of the less academically minded young people and are too detached from working life and the problems of industry. There is a fairly extensive body of research which gives support to some of these claims, especially the criticism levelled at the last few years of compulsory schooling[2].

However, caution needs to be exercised in interpreting the evidence, both of employers' attitudes and of the problems resulting from the inadequacies of the educational system. In the case of employers' attitudes it is important to ask not simply what employers feel, but also to assess to what extent the views expressed suggest a change from the past, for if we are seeking to explain a rise in the level of youth unemployment, views that do not reflect a change over time, no matter how damning in themselves, will be less persuasive. In this context it is interesting to review the answers of employers in the survey quoted above to such a question. When asked whether they thought that the calibre of young people coming to them for jobs had improved or declined in the past five years, almost two thirds said that there had been no change or an improvement: less than a third said that there had been a decline. Of course, the timescale covered by this question was relatively short. Many of the comments made about a change in the attitude and personal qualities of young people imply a comparison with earlier generations rather than with young people five years ago. Nevertheless, the timescale has some relevance as it covers a period when a significant rise occurred in the level of youth unemployment.

If we turn to the criticisms of the level and type of education received by young people then similar comments might be made. It is less easy to show a deterioration in such matters than it is simply to point to criticism of the present position. In this context, it is worthwhile noting that suggestions that the educational system does not adequately prepare young people for working life are far from new. More than twenty years ago, the Crowther report commented on the 'abrupt transition from school to work' and noted that 'a good many people have doubts whether school conditions should not be brought for everybody a little nearer to work conditions'[3]. In fact, in recent years attempts have been made to meet these criticisms with increased emphasis on careers guidance, vocational preparation and work sampling experiments. This is not to suggest that the problems frequently noted have been overcome: it is meant to indicate that in recent years at least some attention has been paid to a long-standing problem.

Some commentators have concentrated not just on the way in which employers may find young people unattractive recruits, but also on the claim that young people themselves may not be eager to obtain employment. This claim has two elements. The first is that young people are no longer willing to accept certain kinds of jobs: in particular, the low paid jobs which involve a great deal of repetitive work. Some of the evidence to support this claim is anecdotal but there is also a limited amount of research evidence. Thus, it has been argued

The literature on youth attitudes is scarce but there does seem to be a growing demand for meaningful work and an avoidance of repetitive monotonous tasks. This would imply that youth might be more hesitant than in the past to accept certain kinds of jobs which would further imply an increase in youth unemployment rates[4].

On the other hand it can also be argued that the research in this area has not established that the crucial division on such matters is an age one: after all there is a large body of literature on job satisfaction and the quality of working life which shows a more general concern with the current nature of employment in industry. Similarly, research in France has shown a considerable variation in attitudes among young people on such matters according to sex, social origin, education, training and the like[5]. It is also clear that in practice in many cases well qualified young people are lowering their employment expectations and accepting jobs that they would have rejected previously[6].

The second element to the claim that young people are less willing than they were to accept certain kinds of work suggests that they are able to adopt this attitude because unemployment is not such a frightening prospect as it used to be. The suggestion made is that young people are cushioned from the worst economic effects of unemployment because they are able to rely on their families for support (though as was argued in Chapter 1 with unemployment increasingly affecting whole families, rather than just young people, this line of argument may be less persuasive) and, possibly more importantly, because of the benefits they receive from the state. A number of studies that have looked at unemployment in general have supported this latter proposition. For example, an OECD study of ten countries[7] found that in seven of them increasing the level of unemployment benefits could have led to a rise in voluntary unemployment. Similarly a study of the effect of the introduction of the earnings related supplements in Britain by Maki and Spindler[8] suggested that the average rate of unemployment between 1967 and 1972 would have been 0.6 per cent lower had the supplement not been available. However, that particular study has been criticised by others[9] for exaggerating the impact of the earnings related supplement and more generally Showler[10] has suggested that any link that can be established between unemployment benefits and the level of

unemployment is restricted to the late 1960s and
early 1970s and cannot be shown for later years.
The research referred to above concerned unemployment in general rather than youth unemployment
in particular. There is reason to believe that
the position with respect to young people may be
different in some respects because many of them
cannot claim the full range of state benefits when
unemployed but have to rely on Supplementary
Benefit. It is worthwhile looking then at the
relationship between the pay of young people in
work and the level of support they have been able
to claim from Supplementary Benefit. Table 3.1
looks at this and suggests that there has been
very little change at all in the relationship in
recent years. It needs to be pointed out that
this table only considers gross pay. If one
wanted a precise measure of the extent to which
state financial support for the young unemployed
matched the likely financial benefit from work one
would need to modify these figures: one would
need to take account, for example, of deductions
from gross earnings, the costs of travelling to
employment and the like. In practice, it is
impossible to offer a precise figure, but, at
least, two comments might be made. First,
although state support for the young when unemployed on average would be greater than 20 to 25
per cent of the financial benefit they could
expect from work, it would still be considerably
less than 100 per cent of that figure. An
earlier study which attempted to take deductions
from earnings into account suggested that
Supplementary Benefits for young people might on
average equal about 25 to 30 per cent of net
earnings[11]. Second, it has been argued[12]
that the desire of the unemployed to find work is
not simply a reflection of an economic calculation. While such calculations may be important
other factors are taken into account, including,
for example, the social status associated with
work.

Demographic and Related Changes

In Britain, as in most other Western nations,
there was an increase in the birth rate in the
late 1950s and 1960s: thus, the number of live
births in Great Britain increased from 768,000 in
1951 to 912,000 in 1961 and to 946,000 in 1966.

Table 3.1:   Supplementary Benefit Rates for Young
             People as a Percentage of Gross Weekly
             Earnings of Young People

	Under 18		18 - 20	
	Males	Females	Males	Females
1972				
1973				
1974	24	28	20	27
1975	24	26	20	27
1976	24	26	20	25
1977	25	27	21	26
1978	25	28	21	27
1979	24	26	20	26
1980	26	24	19	24
1981	24	26	21	25
1982	24	27	21	26

Note: Earnings figures for April each year from
          New Earnings Survey.   Supplementary
          Benefits scale rate for relevant age
          group at same date.   Earnings figures
          are gross rather than net and therefore
          percentage figures in table are an
          estimate of real benefit and
          supplementary benefit payments, but are
          consistently stated.

Sources: Social Security Statistics for relevant
          years New Earnings Survey for relevant
          years.

The birth rate fell back again towards the end of the 1960s: in 1971 there were 870,000 live births and by 1981 only 703,000. These changes in the birth rate had an effect on the number of young people able to enter the labour market. In the 1970s the number of young people reaching the statutory minimum school leaving age started to increase: Table 3.2 shows that the number of people in the 15 to 19 age range rose by over 900,000 between 1970 and 1982 (and this age range as a proportion of the total population increased from 6.9 per cent to 8.4 per cent). The number of people in this age range will start to decline in the 1980s as a reflection of the lower birth rates of the 1970s, particularly the mid 1970s (although the number of births in 1982 was well below the 1971 level, in fact, the birth rate was still well above that in the mid 1970s). It has been argued that the rise in the size of the 15 - 19 age group in the 1970s has been one of the reasons for the increase in the level of youth unemployment over the same period.

Superficially, there is much that is attractive about this view. However, a number of reservations need to be noted. First an increase in the size of the 15 - 19 age group does not necessarily lead to a matching increase in the number of young people entering the labour force. Many young people enter the labour force when they reach the statutory minimum school leaving age, but many do not, and the proportions change from year to year. In fact, the proportion of young people staying on at school or entering full time education has risen over the 1970s and while this has by no means cancelled out the impact of the demographic trends on the labour force, it has blunted them. It also needs to be remembered that the proportion of the 15 to 19 age group entering the labour market was affected significantly in 1972 with the raising of the statutory minimum school leaving age. This removed 15 year olds from the labour market and meant that 15 to 19 year olds accounted for a smaller proportion of the economically active population in succeeding years than they had done before the raising of the school leaving age, despite the fact that the crude numbers of people in the 15 to 19 age range was rising.

A second reservation that needs to be mentioned about the effect of demographic changes, is

The Causes of Youth Unemployment

Table 3.2:   Age distribution of population U.K.
             1970 - 1982

	Number of persons (thousands) aged:		
	Under 1 year	15-19	All ages
1970	878	3,829	55,421
1971	845	3,841	55,610
1972	846	3,896	55,781
1973	795	3,958	55,913
1974	739	4,024	55,922
1975	708	4,119	55,901
1976	678	4,228	55,886
1977	645	4,331	55,852
1978	656	4,124	55,836
1979	711	4,529	55,881
1980	734	4,620	55,945
1981	729	4,735	56,348
1982	711	4,746	56,340

Note: All mid-year estimates
          1981, 1982 figures are provisional.

Source: Annual Abstract of Statistics, 1982, p.13.
          Annual Abstratc of Statistics, 1984, p.11.

that an increase in the supply of labour from a particular age group does not necessarily have to lead to an increase in the level of unemployment: clearly, the level of demand for labour is crucial in this context. If the level of demand is high or increasing then the kind of demographic changes that have been reviewed need not lead to higher unemployment. In this context it is worthwhile noting that the number of young people in the population has also increased in earlier periods (for example, from 1959 to the mid 1960s) and such increases have not always been accompanied by a rise in the level of youth unemployment. Similarly, it has been noted that the U.S.A. had much greater success than Britain in dealing with the same kind of demographic changes in the 1970s. 'During the 1970s the proportion of the American labour force under the age of 25 increased by more than one-third, but the gap between unemployment rates for youth and the rest of the labour force was actually reduced.'[13]

The argument that the high level of youth unemployment is a consequence of demographic changes has some similarities to the suggestion that the level of youth unemployment is a reflection of another change in the supply side of the labour market, the increase in the number of women in employment or seeking employment. Table 3.3 shows that over the last two decades the proportion of women in work or actively seeking work has risen markedly; this has been particularly so in the case of women over 25 and under 60. It has been argued that this increase in the number of women in the labour market has meant that younger people have had to face greater competition for employment than in the past. Of course, in practice not all jobs are equally open to those seeking employment and women will not always be competing for work with young people. Nevertheless, in many cases direct competition can be noted, particularly in the service sector where both women and young people are strongly represented. Probably the strongest competition can be found within this sector between females of different ages. However, it is important to note that overall female activity rates started to stabilise in the late 1970s: they rose by only 0.3 per cent between 1976 and 1981 whereas in the previous five years they had risen by 4.2 per cent. At the same time male economic activity

Table 3.3 Economic activity rates: by age and sex 1961 - 1981

	16-19²	20-24	25-44	45-54/59³	55-59/60-64⁴	60/65+⁵	All aged 16 or over
Married females							
1961	41.0	41.3	33.6	36.1	26.4	7.3	29.7
1971	41.6	45.7	46.4	57.0	45.5	14.2	42.2
1976	52.5	57.6	56.8	64.8	51.2	12.6	49.0
1979	50.9	57.8	58.7	65.6	52.1	10.1	49.6
1981	48.9	50.8	58.5	58.8	51.9	11.5	49.9
Non-married females							
1961	73.2	89.4	84.2	75.3	61.9	11.4	50.6
1971	57.2	81.2	80.4	78.1	67.2	11.0	43.7
1976	68.0	76.2	79.1	77.3	66.4	8.4	43.1
1979	65.9	78.1	78.4	76.7	63.8	5.3	42.8
1981	65.8	78.4	76.9	76.5	63.1	5.9	43.6
All females							
1961	71.1	62.0	40.8	44.0	37.1	9.7	37.4
1971	55.9	60.1	50.6	60.6	51.1	12.4	42.1
1976	66.6	65.7	59.9	66.9	55.0	10.2	46.9
1979	64.8	67.9	61.8	67.5	54.9	7.4	47.0
1981	64.5	68.0	61.6	68.5	54.7	8.3	47.2
All males							
1961	74.6	91.9	98.2	99.2	91.2	24.4	86.0
1971	60.9	89.9	97.9	96.8	86.6	19.4	81.4
1976	72.6	89.0	97.6	96.5	83.0	14.4	80.7
1979	70.7	88.3	97.4	95.2	75.8	10.2	78.6
1981	72.7	88.2	97.2	94.4	72.0	10.3	78.1

rates fell, though in this case the fall was simply a continuation of earlier trends. Undoubtedly stabilisation of the female economic activity rates has been a consequence of the reduction in employment opportunities and the resultant decision by women to withdraw from the labour market, probably temporarily. The impact, though, if the reductions in both the male and female economic activity rates are taken into account is worthwhile noting for it suggests that the rise in youth unemployment cannot simply be the result of increased competition in the labour market from other age ranges, and in particular from females over 25 years of age. Of course, this is a general statement and does not preclude an argument that, say, the rise in female economic activity rates may have had an impact on employment opportunities in certain parts of the labour market. This particular issue will be referred to again later in the chapter.

Relative Wage Costs

One of the arguments frequently advanced in the recent political debate on unemployment generally, but also on youth unemployment in particular, is that the unemployed have been 'pricing themselves out of work' by demanding wages that are too high. As far as the particular case of youth unemployment is concerned it has been argued that one of the reasons for the rise in the rate is that young people have been earning relatively higher wages than in the past. This means, the argument proceeds, that employers have been less likely to offer them work in preference to older people. In 1981, Jim Prior, Secretary of State for Employment, said in the House of Commons: 'One of the problems with young workers and growing unemployment among young people is that over the past few years young workers have started to price themselves out of jobs. There is no doubt about that'[10].

Table 3.4 summarises the movements in young people's earnings relative to those of older workers[11]. From this table it can be seen that young people's earnings did rise as a proportion of those gained by older workers in the early 1970s. However, by the mid 1970s this trend had been halted and eventually in the early 1980s was reversed. The result is that although in most

Table 3.4:   Average gross weekly earnings of full-
             time employees under 21 whose pay was
             not affected by absence as a percent-
             age of the corresponding figure for
             those aged 21 and over

	Males		Females	
	18-20	under 18	18-20	under 18
1970	56	31	71	49
1971	-	-	-	-
1972	-	-	-	-
1973	-	-	-	-
1974	60	38	75	56
1975	62	41	74	58
1976	61	39	73	54
1977	61	40	74	55
1978	61	40	74	54
1979	61	40	75	56
1980	61	39	73	55
1981	59	39	71	53
1982	63	39	70	52
1983	58	36	69	49

Note: April each year, based on New Earnings
           Survey dates.

Source: Hansard, Written Answers for 21 December
           1982, pp 280-1
           New Earnings Survey, 1982, 1983.

cases young people's earnings represented a higher
proportion of older workers earnings in 1983 than
they did in 1970 in all of the categories examined
in Table 3.4 the proportion was also lower in 1983
than it had been in 1975.

It could be argued, with justification, that
the costs of employing a young rather than an
older person, are not fully reflected if only
average earnings are taken into account.
Employers also have insurance and pensions payments and they like to make and may have to
provide training as well as a variety of social
and recreational benefits. Clearly the extent of
such additional costs will vary from employer to
employer, though, it is not unreasonable to
suggest that they are likely to be a higher
proportion of young than older people's earnings,
if only because of the structure of insurance
payments and the greater likelihood that younger
workers will need training. This means that the
costs of employing a younger worker may be greater
than implied by Table 3.3: such assessments as
can be made, though, would not suggest that an
analysis of costs rather than earnings would
produce markedly different trends.

Two further points need to be made about
changes in the costs of employing young workers
and the effect this might have on the level of
unemployment. First, the relative earnings of
young people have been affected by changes in the
composition of that group as well as changes in
the level of earnings of the people concerned.
For example, the raising of the school leaving age
in 1972, and the removal of 15 year olds from the
labour market significantly changed the composition of the under 18 and the under 21 age
groups. In many industries wages are directly
related to age as far as young people are concerned, so that the removal of 15 year olds by
itself would have significantly increased the
average wage for, say, the under 18s or the under
21 year olds. It has been estimated that the
raising of the school leaving age might have added
at least five per cent to the average earnings of
the under 21 age group[12].

The second point concerns the likely impact of
an increase in the relative cost of employing
young people. It has already been noted that
relative earnings of young people increased in the
early 1970s and that in practice it is reasonable

to assume that costs increased in a similar proportion. If we examine the position prior to the 1970s then although there were important fluctuations and there was not simply one consistent trend, one can identify a number of occasions when the relative costs of employing young people rose, particularly the mid 1960s. However, even if these increases are taken into account, as well as the ones noted for the early 1970s, it is still possible to argue that they would not represent a significant element in a total wage bill of a typical employer.

In the case of young males, the earnings of males aged under 21 increased as a percentage of adult male earnings by ten percentage points between 1966 and 1976. If, however, we take an average employer with an all-male labour force comprised of ten per cent young males and 90 per cent adult males, the pay of young males would have made up about five per cent of his total wage bill in 1966 (when young male earnings were 50 per cent of adult male earnings), the increase in relative earnings of young males would have increased his wage bill by one percentage point and in terms of total costs this represents an increase of 0.6 per cent. When it is remembered that this magnitude of change was taking place fairly gradually over a ten-year period at the same time as rapid wage inflation, increases in National Insurance and equal pay legislation, it becomes apparent that a small change is dwarfed by other events affecting employers' wage bills[13].

The essential point is that even if the period when the relative costs of employing young people increased is simply considered, and the period (quite a significant period) when they did not do so is ignored, the argument that employers would react to such increases by changing hiring policy assumes a very simple economic view of behaviour and one in which employers have a keen awareness of what must by comparison have been fairly minor changes in one aspect of their costs.

This line of argument would suggest that the relative wages of young people would not be an important part of an explanation of youth unemployment. This, in fact, is the line that has been taken in a number of pieces of research in Britain and elsewhere.[18] However, recent research[19] has modified this view. For example, a paper by Wells followed the argument of Merrilees and Wilson[20] that youth unemployment differed in the pre and post late 1960's period. Relative wages may not have been an important explanation for youth unemployment in the earlier period because young people in the labour force were in short supply 'and the level of their employment (was) determined largely by the size of the relevant demographic cohort and the decision of young people to enter further education or employment'. However, relative wages may have been more important in the later period when there was a surplus of young people in the labour market and 'their employment appears to have been determined both by the general demand for labour and the cost of their labour relative to other groups'.[21] Wells suggested that the relative wage levels of young people was most important as an explanation of unemployment of males under 18 years of age.

Structural Change in Industry

There has been a great deal of discussion in recent years about the consequences of changes in the structure of industry, and the effects of changes in technology, on employment opportunities. In particular, it has been suggested that young people might have suffered disproportionately from such changes and that this might have been one of the causes of the increase in the level of youth unemployment.

It is certainly the case that changes have taken place in the structure of industry over the past couple of decades and that these changes have had an affect on the level of employment. Table 3.5 shows that between 1961 and 1982 the number of employees engaged in a number of industries declined sharply: for instance the primary industries and manufacturing industries (most individual manufacturing industries as well as the overall total). This decline in employment opportunities, to a certain extent, but by no means entirely, was balanced out by an increase in employment in other industries in the service sector. The reductions in employment oppor-

Table 3.5: Employees in Employment: by Industry U.K. 1961-1982

	United Kingdom				Thousands			
	1961	1966	1971	1977	1979	1980	1981	1982
Agriculture, forestry, and fishing	710	580	432	388	367	370	360	354
Mining and quarrying	727	570	396	350	346	344	332	326
Manufacturing:								
Food, drink and tobacco	793	797	770	711	698	681	632	622
Chemicals, coal & petroleum products	499	495	482	472	482	470	432	415
Metal manufacture	643	627	557	483	444	401	326	295
Engineering & allied industries	3,654	3,778	3,615	3,295	3,269	3,121	2,739	2,646
Textile, leather & clothing	1,444	1,319	1,124	914	897	813	707	616
Rest of manufacturing	1,508	1,571	1,511	1,390	1,386	1,322	1,202	1,158
Total manufacturing	8,540	8,587	8,058	7,292	7,176	6,808	6,038	5,752
Construction	1,485	1,648	1,262	1,270	1,292	1,265	1,132	1,049
Gas, electricity & water	389	432	377	347	346	347	340	340
Services:								
Transport & communication	1,678	1,622	1,568	1,468	1,494	1,500	1,440	1,383
Distributive trades	2,767	2,920	2,610	2,753	2,826	2,790	2,635	2,706
Insurance, banking & finance	684	818	976	1,145	1,233	1,258	1,233	1,321
Professional & scientific services	2,124	2,591	2,989	3,647	3,729	3,717	3,695	3,768
Miscellaneous services	1,819	2,066	1,946	2,343	2,493	2,519	2,414	2,554
Public administration	1,311	1,424	1,509	1,615	1,619	1,596	1,579	1,549
Total services	10,382	11,441	11,597	12,970	13,394	13,379	12,996	13,282
All industries & services	22,233	23,257	22,122	22,619	22,920	22,511	21,198	21,103

Note: Figures refer to June of each year
Source: Social Trends, Vol 14, 1984, p 61

tunities can be put down to a number of different factors: in some cases activity and volume has declined but in most improved production or operating techniques have had a major influence. It is difficult though to see how the argument can be sustained that by themselves these changes in the structure of industry have had a major and special effect on the level of youth unemployment because in practice young people have not been concentrated most heavily in the worst affected industries. Table 3.6 shows that manufacturing industries, which have been particularly badly affected in recent years in terms of employment opportunities, have employed relatively few young people. On the other hand, young people are heavily concentrated, more than older workers, in a number of service industries, and these indus-tries have suffered less than others from the loss of employment opportunities, and in some case employment opportunities have been increased.

General Economic Conditions

The arguments examined so far all have assumed that the level of youth unemployment can be explained by reference to the position, attitudes and abilities of the young themselves. The con-trast with this view is the suggestion that the level of youth unemployment, like the level of overall unemployment, is most responsive to general economic conditions. When conditions are boyant employers will demand more labour, and while the increase in demand may bring an increase in supply (economic activity rates may rise because, for example, married women may decide that it is worthwhile trying to find work, or because young people may decide that it is worth-while leaving school earlier than they would have done otherwise) to take advantage of employment opportunities) it is anticipated that the increase in supply will lag behind and be less than the increase in demand. The result will be a reduc-tion in the overall level of unemployment. Young people will benefit from this reduction like others. The reverse will happen when economic conditions worsen. Employers will reduce their labour forces either by cutting back on recruit-ment or by redundancies and young people will suffer in such a situation along with everyone else. In support of this view it can be pointed

Table 3.6: Employment of 16-19 year olds: by sex and industry
Great Britain, 1981

	Male employees		Female employees	
	Aged 16-19	All ages	Aged 16-19	All ages
	(percentages)			
Industry division[1]:				
agriculture, forestry, and fishing	3.3	2.0	0.6	0.8
Energy and water supply industries	3.7	5.4	0.8	1.1
Extraction of minerals and ores other than fuels: manufacture of metals, mineral products & chemicals	3.8	5.9	2.5	2.4
Metal goods, engineering, and vehicles industries	15.6	18.6	6.5	7.0
Other manufacturing industries	11.7	11.9	13.7	11.8
Construction	13.7	8.5	1.0	1.2
Distribution, hotels and catering: repairs	27.0	12.8	35.6	23.3
Transport and communication	4.8	9.1	3.4	2.9
Banking, finance, insurance, business services and leasing	4.7	6.5	14.0	8.9
Other services	11.1	18.2	21.2	39.2
Not identified[2]	0.5	1.1	0.6	1.3
Total in employment (= 100%) (thousands)	898	12,092	834	8,798

[1]Standard Industrial Classification (revised 1980)

[2]Including those in employment outside the United Kingdom

Note: Industry divisions according to standard industrial classification (revised 1980)

Source: Social Trends, Vol 13, 1983, p 190

out that in the past unemployment rates for young
people have moved in the same direction as those
for the labour force as a whole.

This argument, though, normally takes account
of the fact that while young people may benefit
and suffer from changes in general economic
conditions, there are likely to be important
differences in the extent to which particular age
groups are affected, and probably more crucially
the speed with which they are affected. It is
recognised, for example, that unemployment statistics show that in time of depression, especially
in the early stages of the depression, the unemployment rates for young people usually rise
faster than those for other age groups. The
reverse is usually the case when economic conditions improve. In other words, it appears as
though youth unemployment rates are more sensitive
to changes in economic conditions than the overall
unemployment rates.

Two main explanations are offered for this.
The first is that young people are more vulnerable
to cut-backs in recruitment by employers because
proportionately they are more likely to be in the
position of seeking work. This is obviously
particularly the case with school leavers, who are
entering the labour market for the first time.
However, it is also likely to be the case with
other young people because, on average, the young
change their jobs more frequently then older
workers. This can be seen from Table 3.7 which
shows turnover by age. In 1980, between a fifth
and a quarter of all young people under 25 years
of age had changed their employer at least once in
the previous 12 months, compared to an average
figure for the working population as a whole of
about 9 per cent. A proportion of young people
change their jobs even more frequently than might
be implied by these statistics: for example, some
change jobs not just once but a number of times a
year. However, research has suggested[22] that
the "chronic job changers", those who change jobs
on average more frequently than once every six
months, are a small proportion of the age group.
For example, Baxter in a study of young people in
Sheffield[23] estimated that no more than about
3-4 per cent of males and 2-3 per cent of females
surveyed could be classified as chronic job
changers. The more general point, though,
remains: young people tend on average to change

The Causes of Youth Unemployment

Table 3.7: Labour Turnover by Age, Great Britain, 1980

Sex and Age   Changes of Employer in the previous 12 months

Males	Total changing %	Average number of changes per person
16 - 17	24	0.40
18 - 24	21	0.30
25 - 34	11	0.14
35 - 44	7	0.09
45 - 54	4	0.05
55 - 59	3	0.02
60 - 64	1	0.01
65 and over	4	0.04
Total	9	0.12

Females		
16 - 17	26	0.35
18 - 24	21	0.30
25 - 34	12	0.15
35 - 44	10	0.12
45 - 54	7	0.08
55 - 59	3	0.04
60 - 67	4	0.03
65 and over	2	0.01
Total	11	0.14

Source: General Household Survey 1980, p 114

jobs more frequently than older workers. Two explanations have been put forward for this. One is that the "early years of employment are when young people decide on what jobs they want to do and so frequently job changing is regarded as "job shopping": the other is that 'rather than trying-out jobs, the young person, and especially the least able young person, is 'attempting to relieve the intrinsic boredom of the jobs he or she is able to get while maximising benefits such as pay'[24]. A Manpower Services Commission report [25] argued that in practice both explanations have some validity with the second, as is suggested in the above formulation, being most applicable for less qualified young people. It is worthwhile noting that the high job mobility of young people is not confined to Britain but has been commented on by researchers in a number of different countries. Researchers in the USA[26] have noted that young people do not only change jobs frequently but also are likely to move into and out of the labour market frequently: it has been suggested that teenagers in particular are likely to move rapidly between the three labour force states of employment, unemployment and non-participation.

The second explanation for the sensitivity of young people to changes in economic conditions concerns policies on redundancy. It is suggested that young people are likely to be particularly vulnerable when an employer declares redundancies. This may be because, frequently with the agreement of, if not under pressure from, trade unions, employers adopt a policy of "last in, first out". It also needs to be recognised that the redundancy payments legislation, which provides for compensation to be linked to length of service and age, means that often it is in an employers own interest to make younger rather than older workers redundant, if such a choice is necessary. The evidence on this contention is more patchy than it is on the issue of job changing. Cases can be quoted where a policy of "last in, first out" has been adopted and the implications of redundancy payments legislation are easy to appreciate. However, while the costs of making a young person redundant may be less than attempting the same exercise with an older worker, in some cases the costs of keeping the younger worker in employment may be less (because of lower wage levels) and in many cases where voluntary redundancy is requested the nature of the terms offered mean that older workers find the prospect more attractive than younger workers. Further, it needs to be borne in mind that in cases where a factory or plant is closed down all workers, whatever their age, may be made redundant.

The Importance of Different Explanations

A number of studies have tried to assess the importance of different explanations for the rise in the level of youth unemployment, and many, by using regression analysis have been able to examine the relative importance of factors, in combination as well as singly. Some studies have concentrated on the experience of individual countries over a period of time: others have looked at a number of different countries, usually over a shorter time period. While it would be wrong to suggest a firm consensus from these studies, it is possible to argue that there is a strong trend for one particular factor to be high- lighted as being of overriding importance in explainng the causes of youth unemployment. Most studies have suggested that to a large extent youth unemployment is a function of the general level of economic activity and as such that this is by far the most important single explanatory variable. This was the conclusion, for example, of Makeham's study of youth unemployment in Britain[22]. He noted, as one would expect in such an instance, that movements in youth unem- ployment have been closely related to movements in overall unemployment but that the level of youth unemployment has varied more swiftly. Thus, he showed that if the unemployment rate for all males rises by one percentage point, then the unemploy- ment rate for males under 20 (excluding school leavers), rises by about 1.7 percentage points. Similarly, a rise in the unemployment rate for all females of one percentage point leads to an increase in the unemployment rate for young females under 20 (again, excluding school leavers) by almost three percentage points. So far, it appears that the relationship has also held when unemployment has been falling: youth unemployment has fallen faster than overall employment. Makeham made a number of comments about the possible reasons for the greater sensitivity of youth than overall unemployment to changes in the level of economic activity. He confessed that it is 'not possible to disentangle which of the explanations that can be put forward to explain this sensitivity.... is the most significant' but went on to argue that 'it seems likely that cuts in recruitment and changes in the propensity to register are considerable influences'[28].

The emphasis that Makeham placed on the importance of the level of economic activity as an explanation for the level of youth unemployment was echoed by Casson's study of three Western countries, West Germany, Italy and the United Kingdom[29]. Casson's analysis, based on EEC Labour Force Sample surveys, suggested that school leavers would be highly vulnerable during a recession (what he called the "school-leaver hypothesis"), and that the level of youth unemployment could be linked to the amount of job changing in this age group (what he called the "job-search hypothesis"). Another international study, this time by a major international organisation, the Organisation for Economic Co-operation and Development, similarly emphasised the importance of the level of economic activity as an explanation for the level of youth unemployment. Thus, it was stated that the level of aggregate demand 'was consistently the most single important influence on youth unemployment'[30]. A similar conclusion was reached in a study by the International Labour Office. 'There is no single cause of the high rate of youth unemployment. The most significant one, however, is the decline in the number of jobs due to the recession'[31].

It is important to record that while most studies have stressed the importance of the level of general economic activity in explaining the level of youth unemployment, some writers have dissented from this conclusion. In the USA, for example, the work of Feldstein[31] has challenged this view and more recently in Britain a similar degree of scepticism has been shown. For example, Lynch and Richardson concluded that 'changes in business conditions are unlikely to have been the only important determinant of increasing youth unemployment in the last ten years'[33]. Lynch and Richardson went on to argue that youth unemployment 'also seems sensative to the relative cost of employing young workers'[34]. They recognise that such conclusions challenge those of

Makeham's study and have important policy implications. While they accept that their study has certain limitations, nevertheless, they argue that such limitations are less important than there have been in other studies.

> Although the empirical results reported above are generally good or very good by certain statistical criteria, such as goodness of fit, absence of autocorrelation, parameter stability and predictive accuracy, we would not claim they are by any means the last word on the subject. The data are important, the model is simple and may well suffer to some degree from simultaneous equation bias, and some of the results are open to considerable discussion. However, the earlier work in this field has suffered from similar or worse handicaps[35].

A somewhat similar line has been taken by Wells.[36] He also recognises that deficiences remain with the data and consequently that the results of his analysis need to be viewed with caution. However, as was noted earlier, he agreed that more weight needs to be given to the effect of the relative wages of young people when seeking an explanation for youth unemployment and suggests that Makeham's seemingly contradictary conclusion was at least in part the result of the fact that he was looking at an earlier time period when young people were in short supply on the labour market. It needs to be noted, though, that while Wells argued for more emphasis to be placed on the relative wage levels of young people this explanation was more firmly supported by the statistical anlysis for males under 18 years of age than for other groups and he accepted that youth unemployment also is strongly associated with changes in the general level of employment.

It is also important to record that no study of youth unemployment, has argued that it can be accounted for simply by reference to the level of general economic activity. For example, while Makeham's study, as was noted earlier, stressed the importance of the level of economic activity, it also recognised that certain other factors need to be taken into account. Makeham argued, for instance, that the economic activity rate of adult females seems to have been an important factor influencing the unemployment rate of young females: in essence, he claimed that some girls may have been displaced in the labour market by the influx of adult women. Makeham also argued that demographic factors seem to have been particularly important as part of the explanation for the rate of school leaver unemployment. Similar comments could be made about the explanations offered by some of the other authors referred to earlier. Thus, Casson, concurred with Makeham's view of the importance of the female economic activity rate, and mentioned other factors like the concentration of young people in seasonal trades, and the phenomenon of young people often obtaining low-wage jobs when they leave school but switching out of them later on.

Conclusion

It would clearly be wrong, then, to suggest that youth unemployment can be explained simply by reference to one factor. Nevertheless, it can be argued that there is wide if not universal agreement that one factor has been particularly important, that is, the level of general economic activity. This does not mean that other factors like demographic changes, the rise in the female economic activity rate, the character and attitude of the young and particularly the relative level of young people's wages have been discounted by all authors, but it means that most see the level of general economic activity as being the most critical.

This conclusion is important, not simply because it locates youth unemployment centrally as part of the more general problem of low economic activity and high overall unemployment, but also because it has implications for remedial action and the likely consequences of policy initiatives.

In the next chapter attention centres on these policy responses. The range of measures introduced to try to reduce the level of youth unemployment are reviewed. Later chapters look at the implications of the responses and at the debate surrounding them.

Notes

1. Quotes in Manpower Services Commission, 1978, Op Cit, p 39.
2. See, for example, P E Willis, Learning to Labour, Saxon House, Farnborough, 1977.
3. Central Advisory Council for Education, 15-18, HMSO, London, 1959, pp 126-8.
4. OECD, Youth Unemployment, Vol 1, OECD, Paris, 1978, pp 43-4.
5. J Rousselet, et al, Les jeunes et l'emploi, Presses Universitaires de France, Paris, 1975.
6. See A Jaffe, J Froomkin, 'Occupational Opportunities for College Education Workers, 1950-1975', Monthly Labour Review, June 1978.
7. Organisation for Economic Co-operation and Development, 'Unemployment Compensation: A Comparison', OECD Observer, November 1978.
8. D Maki, Z A Spindler, 'The Effect of Unemployment Compensation on the Rate of Unemployment in Great Britain', Oxford Economic Papers, Vol 27, November 1975.
9. See, for example, A B Atkinson, J S Fleming, 'Unemployment, Social Security and incentives', Midland Bank Review, Autumn 1978; S Nickell, 'The Effect of Unemployment and Related Benefits on the Duration of Unemployment', Economic Journal, Vol 89, 1979.
10. B Showler, 'Political Economy and Unemployment' in B Showler, A Sinfield (eds), The Workless State, Martin Robertson, Oxford, 1981, pp 27-58.
11. See P Makeham, Youth Unemployment, Research Paper No 10, Department of Employment, HMSO, London, 1980. The price figure quoted varied from 24 per cent to 35 per cent depending on sex and age.
12. For a discussion of this issue see, D Marsden, E Duff Workless - Some Unemployed Men and their Families, Penguin, Harmondsworth, 1975.
13. A Sinfield, What Unemployment Means, Martin Robertson, Oxford, 1981, p 71.
14. Hansard, 28 June 1981.
15. The table compares the earnings of young people under 21 with those of workers aged 21 and over. Other comparisons can be made. For example, in some cases it has argued that for females the comparison should be between those under and those 18 and over, because 18 has been the age at which adult rates have been

paid. The details differ depending on the precise ranges covered but the trends are similar.

16. P Makeham, _Op Cit_, p 7.
17. _Ibid_, p 28.
18. See, for example, Makeham, _Ibid_.
19. See, for example, L Lynch, _Job Search and Youth Unemployment_, Centre for Labour Economics Discussion Paper, No 158, 1983; J Martin _Effects of the Minimum Wage on the Youth Labour Market in North America and France_, OECD, Occasional Studies, 1983.
20. W Merrilees, R Wilson, _Disequilibrium in the Labour Market for Young People in Great Britain_, Manpower Research Group Discussion Paper No 10, Warwick University, 1979.
21. W Wells, _The Relative Pay and Employment of Young People_, Research Paper No 42, Department of Employment, 1983, p 2.
22. There is a fairly wide body of research available on this topic. For example, see: J C Baxter, 'The Chronic Job Changer: A Study of Youth Unemployment', _Social and Economic Administration_, Vol 9, No 3, 1975; N Cherry, 'Persistent Job Changing - Is it a Problem?' _Journal of Occupational Psychology_, 1976; Manpower Services Commission, _Young People and Work_, Manpower Studies, No 19781, HMSO, London, 1978.
23. J L Baxter, _Ibid_.
24. Manpower Services Commission, 1978, _Op Cit_, p 48.
25. _Ibid_.
26. K B Clark, L H Summers, 'The Dynamics of Youth Unemployment"' in R B Freeman, D Wise (eds) National Bureau of Economic Research Conference on Youth Unemployment, 1980.
27. _Op Cit_.
28. _Ibid_, p 41.
29. M Casson, _Youth Unemployment_, Macmillan, London, 1979.
30. OECD, _Youth Unemployment: The Causes and Consequences_, OECD, Paris, 1980, p 8.
31. P Melvyn, _Youth Unemployment: Roots and Remedies_, World Employment Programme Research, Working Paper, ILO, Geneve, 1977, p 4.
32. M Feldstein, _Lowering and Permanent Rate of Unemployment_, US Congress, Joint Economic Committee, Washington, USA, 1973.

33. L M Lynch, R Richardson, 'Unemployment of Young Workers in Britain', British Journal of Industrial Relations, Vol XX, No 3, November 1982, p 369.
34. Ibid, p 369.
35. Ibid, p 370-1.
36. Op Cit.

Chapter Four

YOUTH UNEMPLOYMENT: A REVIEW OF POLICY MEASURES

In the last two chapters we have sought to examine
the extent of unemployment amongst young people
and the explanations put forward for it. In this
chapter it is intended to examine the way Governments have responded with policy initiatives to
the rise in youth unemployment, particularly since
the mid-1970s.

The traditional response to rising unemployment in the post Second World War years in most
Western nations was for governments to take action
designed to increase demand in the economy. However, in the early 1970s a wide spectrum of
opinion decided that such a response was too
dangerous, because of the potential consequences
for inflation. It is important to stress that
this view was not simply held by those often
referred to as "monetarists" but that it extended
to a much wider body of opinion. Governments,
then, began to search for other ways of dealing
with high and rising unemployment which might have
more acceptable consequences for inflation. The
policies proposed and introduced frequently are
referred to as "special employment measures".

The special employment measures introduced in
Britain had much in common with those introduced
in other countries: in some cases they were the
direct result of studies of the provisions elsewhere. Generally, such measures were targetted on
particular groups and were seen to have a low net
public expenditure cost. The aim was to help the
unemployed but to affect the rest of the economy
as little as possible. The measures introduced
designed to affect youth unemployment can be
divided into three categories: subsidies, job
creation and training. In addition measures were

also introduced which it was felt might help to reduce the size of the active labour force and as a result indirectly benefit the young as well as others.

Subsidies

A range of employment subsidies were introduced in the 1970s though many of them were not targetted on the young; in some cases the young were explicitly excluded from the provisions. Nevertheless, a number of subsidies aimed at the young have been introduced since the mid 1970s. The first of these, the Recruitment Subsidy for School Leavers, was introduced in 1975. It provided a subsidy of £5 a week for 6 months to employers who recruited young people under 20 years old when normally they would not have done so. The first subsidy had a relatively short history. It was abandoned in 1976, although it was replaced by the Youth Employment Subsidy designed to continue until 1978. This had similar aims, but the details were different: it offered employers a subsidy of £10 a week for up to 26 weeks if they provided a job for a young person under 20 who had been unemployed continuously for the previous 6 months.

The idea of subsidies to encourage the recruitment of young people was revived in 1981. In July of that year the Prime Minister announced in the House of Commons plans to introduce a new provision, the Young Workers Scheme. Under the terms of this provision a weekly payment of £15 was offered to employers who took on a young person under 18 years of age provided that they were in their first year of work and provided that their earnings were below £40 a week: if they earned over £40 a week but under £45 then the subsidy was halved. Whatever the level, the subsidy itself was designed to last for 1 year. The precise earnings levels have been altered since the introduction of the subsidy (in June 1983 it was announced that they were being raised from 1 August to £42 for the full subsidy and £47 for the half subsidy) but the general approach has been maintained. The introduction of this subsidy proved to be particularly controversial because of the maximum earnings stipulation: it was seen by some as a way of encouraging low wages and on this basis was opposed by the trade union movement.

Job Creation

Employment subsidies, certainly as far as the young have been concerned, have been much less important than job creation. The history of job creation can be traced back well beyond the post Second World War years. Job creation schemes, for example, were used in Britain, as well as in many other countries, extensively in the 1930s. Probably their most controversial use was in Germany before the Second World War, and this experience coloured the attitude of many to the use of such devices subsequently. However, it is reasonable to argue that the measures introduced in the post Second World War years, starting in the USA in the 1960s, in Canada a few years later, and that spread throughout Western Europe in the 1970s, were substantially different from the earlier schemes. Much more emphasis was placed on the quality of the work done, on the direct value of such work for the community and on improvement of the work skills of those who took part.

The first of the new generation of British job creation schemes, Community Industry, was introduced in 1972 following an initiative taken the previous year by a number of voluntary and statutory agencies with responsibility for the young. The aim was to provide help for two groups of young people: those who found it difficult to obtain employment because of their social and economic background and those of above average ability who were in jobs that gave them little satisfaction or interest.

Community Industry was started as an experiment in six areas which had 'development' or 'intermediate' status. The Government gave financial support although the schemes themselves were run by the National Association of Youth Clubs. The pilot schemes were reviewed in 1972 and the Government decided that they should be continued renewing its financial support. However, the aims of Community Industry were modified and narrowed. The new aims were stated in the following way:

> The broad aim shall be to assist young people to cope more effectively with life in society, both in terms of overcoming personal problems and by making a positive contribution to their communities. The particular aim of the scheme shall be to

prepare for regular employment (in as short a time as practicable) unemployed young people who for various reasons find it more difficult than their contemporaries to obtain and keep jobs, with special emphasis on the needs of those who are socially or personally disadvantaged. The method of operation shall take the form of work experience in full time but temporary employment embodying a style of working which is industrially realistic and capable of turning out productions economically to the standard of quality required by sponsors. The work situation shall be used to develop the educational and vocational potential of each young employee so that:

(i)   his standard of skill, basic knowledge and social attitude can be advanced to the extent that given the opportunity he could be taken on in other full-time employment.

(ii)   experience of work in the scheme will lead to a more positive responsible attitude to society.

(iii)   through the experience of participating in the organisation of the work project in which he is engaged he may gain social organisation skill of wider community application[1].

In practice, important changes had been made to Community Industry. The target group had been defined much more tightly as those who were experiencing difficulty in the employment market because of 'personal problems'. Community Industry no longer was to be seen also as a way of helping those with over-average ability in less demanding jobs. It was to be seen, quite specifically, then, as a form of rehabilitation; as an attempt to improve the personal qualities of the long term young unemployed. It was also clear that Community Industry was not to be seen primarily as a device aimed to help school leavers, for it was to be targeted on those who had already experienced lengthy periods of unemployment.

Community Industry was to be run by a National Management Board, which included representatives from the TUC, CBI, Youth Associations and the Department of Employment amongst its members. Management teams were formed, covering particular geographical areas, to run projects. The management teams included specialists in various aspects of the work and organised projects, though the projects themselves normally were to be under the direct supervision of a consultant with the particular skills needed for the project. Industrial projects were meant to last for a year although in many cases this maximum was exceeded. In practice some people stayed with Community Industry for more than 3 years. Normally the participants were paid a wage in line with what would have been expected for that kind of work.

Community Industry was gradually extended throughout the mid 1970s so that by 1977 forty-two different geographical areas were covered. The numbers engaged in the programme also were increased: by 1977 4,500 young people were being dealt with, making a cumulative total of 11,000 since its inception. Government financial contributions were similarly increased so that by 1977 they were giving £6 million (other financial support, in 1977 amounting to over £1 million, came from the European Social Fund).

In the late 1970s and early 1980s Britain's job creation offerings were subject to a number of reviews. These reviews were not concerned primarily with Community Industry, but centred on the other job creation programmes, which will be outlined later. Nevertheless, Community Industry was considered generally sympathetically. For example, the Holland report[2] gave support to the work being undertaken through Community Industry and as a result it was recommended that the number of places available should be increased. Plans were made for an increase from 5,500 to 7,000 places for 1979-80, though in fact a reduction of the grant in June 1979 meant that the number of places had to be reduced to 6,000. The survival of Community Industry, through the 1970s and into the 1980s is in marked contrast to the fate of the other British job creation programmes, though it has remained a relatively small scale endeavour (in 1982, for example, only 7,000 places were available).

It is important to stress though, that while Community Industry can be seen as the first and most enduring of the current generation of British job creation measures, in many ways it has been a very special one working at the edge of this category. Its emphasis on dealing with young people facing personal as well as labour market problems has meant that it has not been seen as a measure simply designed for a period of rising unemployment. The young people engaged on Community Industry might have faced labour market problems even if the economic climate had been healthier, though no doubt the economic conditions of the 1970s and early 1980s made their position even more difficult.

Community Industry began to be overshadowed from the mid 1970s by the major British job creation programmes. The first of these, called specifically, the Job Creation Programme, was introduced in 1975. Initially it was due to last for two years and was allocated £30 million (to produce 15,000 jobs). The programme was directed by the Manpower Services Commission and, its broad aims were set out in a formal agreement between the Commission and the Secretary of State.

The broad aim of the scheme shall be to provide short-term jobs of social value for those unemployed persons who would particularly benefit and be willing to undertake such work. In operating the Scheme the Commission will seek to promote the establishment and carrying out of the projects by sponsors which will provide temporary, worth-while jobs in areas of high unemployment and will endeavour to:

(a) pay particular attention to the needs of young unemployed persons, take account of training requirements whenever applicable and ensure that the education service is invited to contribute as fully as possible.

(b) give priority, where practicable, to projects which will assist urban renewal.

(c) seek the active co-operation of local authorities and Health Service authorities in the sponsorship of projects in the personal social services and other fields; and

(d) encourage other public bodies (including the nationalised industries), private employers, voluntary organisations, charities and community groups to sponsor suitable projects[3].

This statement illustrates a number of the central features of the Job Creation Programmes. For example, the Programme was explicitly designed to undertake tasks that would be of direct benefit to the community at large, such as by improving the local environment or by assisting in the solution of social or community problems. Similarly, it was made clear that wherever possible participation in a scheme should mean that new skills could be learnt that would be of benefit in finding a normal job afterwards. The Job Creation Programme was not meant to be a training endeavour but its emphasis on improving the skills of those participating in it was important and, as noted earlier, was one of the things that marked it off from the job creation measures of the 1930s.

Later more detailed guidelines were produced to govern the operation of the programme. Target groups were identified: priority was to be given to projects which involved young people (16-24 year olds), although older people, particularly those aged 50 and over could be engaged, especially in a supervisory capacity. Rules were also laid down in an attempt to prevent Job Creation projects being used simply as a substitution for work that would normally have been completed anyway, and it was made clear that the support of interested parties, like trade unions, should be sought.

The programme was run at a local level by ten Area Action Committees which were formed from representatives of trade unions, employers and local authorities, (with an independent chairman). These Action Committees had the responsibility of approving and overseeing individual projects. The majority of the costs of the projects themselves were met by the Manpower Services Commission: they gave a grant to cover wages, insurance contributions and certain administrative costs. The people employed on the projects were to be paid the "wage for the job", subject to certain restrictions, and were to be recruited from the "unemployed" by the main public employment placing agencies.

The detailed provisions of the Job Creation Programme were changed on a number of occasions after its introduction in 1975. A number of specifications were changed: for example, about the age ranges and geographical areas to be covered and the maximum length of projects. Additional sums of money were also assigned to the Programme (an extra £10 million at the end of 1975, a further £65 million at various times throughout 1976, and another £61 million in 1977) and the numbers to be engaged on projects were increased.

Table 4.1 summarises the characteristics of the Job Creation Programme, as at 1976 and 1977. It shows an increase in the number of projects and participants over the period covered. It also shows the extent to which sponsorship of projects was dominated by the public sector.

Of course, this was almost inevitable given the original stipulation that projects should produce something of benefit to the community at large. In practice, many projects were in the constrution or environmental improvement area though the proportion of projects from this area declined over the life of the programme. Most participants were aged under 25 (though about a quarter were between 25 and 49 in 1977 reflecting a change in the guidelines for projects to allow more people who had experienced long-term unemployment but did not fall into the original age ranges to be taken on) and most participants were male.

In terms of the numbers covered, the Job Creation Programme was the most important of such measures in Britain in the mid 1970s. However, a year after its introduction it was joined by the Work Experience Programme. This programme was less extensive in its own right but was to form the basis for a major future initiative. There were some broad similarities between the Job Creation and Work Experience Programmes, in that they both aimed to provide short-term employment opportunities for those out of work. There were, though, also important differences between the programmes. The Work Experience Programme placed

Table 4.1: Selected Characteristics of Job
Creation Programme Projects and
Participants

| | 1976 | | 1977 | |
	First Half %	Second Half %	First Half %	Second Half %
Number of Projects	2,665	3,053	3,472	4,051
Number of Participants	29,262	28,525	30,149	34,281
Project Sponsors				
Local Authority	64	54	51	51
Other Public Body	9	7	7	7
Private Employer/ Tradesmen	3	3	4	8
Voluntary/ Charitable Organisations	23	36	38	35
TOTAL	100	100	100	100
Type of Activity				
Construction	15	16	151	16
Environmental Improvement	36	28	28	23
Production/ Manufacturing	1	1	2	3
Education/ Information	19	21	18	21
Social/ Health Services	16	14	9	12
Research Surveys	10	11	14	12
Other Activities	3	9	14	13
TOTAL	100	100	100	100
Participants				
Males	81	72	78	71
Females	19	28	22	29
TOTAL	100	100	100	100
Aged 16-18	53	43	37	38
19-24	25	31	32	33
25-49	15	19	24	23
50+	7	7	7	6
TOTAL	100	100	100	100

Source: Department of Employment Gazette, March
1977, p 214.

most emphasis on providing an experience that would enhance the job skills of participants and thereby increase their chances in the labour market, whereas the Job Creation Programme placed most emphasis on undertaking work that would be of benefit to the community at large. It was intended that Work Experience projects should offer participants an introduction to a number of different kinds of work as well as a programme of training or further education, probably through a day-release scheme.

In some ways the Work Experience Programme stood mid-way between the Job Creation Programme and Community Industry. It emphasised the development of personal qualities, like increasing self-confidence and was designed to provide a general introduction to working life, as well as the development of specific work skills, aims not dissimilar to those of Community Industry. However, it did not restrict entry to those with "personal problems" in the way that Community Industry did: it had a broad recruitment limited mainly by age (16 to 18 year olds).

The Work Experience Programme, like the Job Creation Programme, was under the overall direction of and funded from the Manpower Services Commission. Its administration, though, was left to eight area offices that were staffed by personnel drawn from within the employment service. These officials were given the power to approve projects proposed by potential sponsors subject to the overall national guidelines. People who participated in projects were given an allowance, not "the rate for the job" as was the case with the Job Creation Programme.

Table 4.2 summarises the characteristics of the Work Experience Programme. The majority of places were provided by sponsors from the private sector, a substantial proportion in the service sector, though about a quarter were in manufacturing industry. The emphasis on the private sector was the reverse of the Job Creation Programme and to an extent was a reflection of the different objectives of the two measures. Again, unlike the Job Creation Programme, the Work Experience Programme engaged a majority of girls (partly because of the nature of tasks available on the projects) and participants were from a very narrow age range.

Table 4.2: Selected Characteristics of Work Experience Programme Projects and Participants

	4th Quarter 1976	1st Quarter 1977	2nd Quarter 1977	3rd Quarter 1977	4th Quarter 1977	Total end '77
Project Sponsors						
Number of Places	6,615	8,743	6,624	9,984	9,712	44,351
	%	%	%	%	%	%
Private Company	77.8	65.9	83.6	81.3	85.2	78.2
Local Authority	14.0	18.9	7.4	9.8	6.1	11.3
Nationalised Industry	3.2	6.2	0.8	1.9	2.4	2.8
Others	5.0	9.0	8.2	6.9	6.3	7.3
TOTAL	100.0	100.0	100.0	100.0	100.0	100.0
Type of Activity						
Manufacturing	25.4	25.1	26.6	24.6	26.1	26.0
Distributive Trades	32.9	20.3	29.6	27.8	26.6	26.5
Other Services	29.2	40.5	33.5	35.9	31.3	34.2
Other Industries	12.5	14.1	10.3	11.7	16.0	13.2
TOTAL	100.0	100.0	100.0	100.0	100.0	100.0

Table 4.2: Selected Characteristics of Work Experience Programme Projects and Participants (continued)

Participants Number of participants joining	2,761	4,800	8,713	14,704	16,593	4,757
	%	%	%	%	%	%
Male	35.0	45.3	46.3	43.9	43.4	43.8
Female	65.0	54.7	53.7	56.0	56.4	56.1
TOTAL	100.0	100.0	100.0	100.0	100.0	100.0
Aged 16	57.0	47.7	73.9	77.7	63.0	67.6
17	30.5	40.1	20.7	17.7	28.8	25.1
18	12.2	12.0	5.2	4.4	7.8	6.9
Non-stated	0.3	0.2	0.3	0.2	0.4	0.3
TOTAL	100.0	100.0	100.0	100.0	100.0	100.0

Source: Department of Employment Gazette, March 1978, pp 295-6

The Job Creation and Work Expereience Programmes had given places to about 120,000 and 40,000
people respectively by 1978 when they were brought
to an end.   Discussions on revisions to the
British job creation measures, in fact, were
started in 1976 almost as soon as the first round
of programmes was in operation.   The Manpower
Services Commission established a working party
under Geoffrey Holland to review the area and make
recommendations.   The working party included
representatives from a variety of non-government
organisations, like the Confederation of British
Industries, the Trades Union Congress, and the
Institute of Careers Officers as well as representatives from relevant Government departments.
The assumption behind the original programmes
had been that they should be temporary measures
because the problem they were meant to deal with
was temporary.   It had been felt that high levels
of unemployment were a reaction to the oil crisis
and that they would decline within a relatively
short time.   Not everyone shared these assumptions but they were widely proclaimed by official
spokesmen.   Such assumptions were less appealing,
though, by the late 1970s and the Holland Commitee
explicitly adopted the view that youth unemployment should not be treated as a short-term but at
least as a medium-term phenomenon.   The Committee
did not predict a particular level of youth
unemployment in the future but suggested that it
was likely to be between 180,000 and 350,000 in
1981.
It was central to the argument produced by the
Committee that one of the main problems with the
then existing job creation programmes was that
they had been introduced on a temporary basis.
This, it said, 'inhibited employers and others,
such as Colleges of Further Education from making
the provisions they could make - and would like to
make - if they could be sure that there was some
commitment for at least two or three years
ahead'[4].
The Committee concluded that the greatest need
was for revision so that provision could be better
ordered and a longer term programme could be outlined.   It suggested that two kinds of opportunities should be introduced for young people.
The first was a range of courses designed to
prepare young people for work: three types were
suggested - assessment or short induction courses,

short industrial courses and remedial or prepara-
tory courses. The second was the provision of
different kinds of work experience: four were
suggested - work experience on employers premises,
project-based work experience, training workshops
and community service. One other important
recommendation was that young people joining such
progammes should be paid an allow- ance, rather
than the 'wage for the job'. It was intended that
together these schemes should provide over 120,000
places at any one time, and, because in many cases
participants would stay for less than a year, they
would deal with about double that number of people
in a year.

The Working Party's report broadly was
accepted by the Government. On 29 June 1977,
Albert Booth, then Secretary of State for Employment, announced that a new Job Creation Programme
would be introduced in the Spring of the following
year. The new programme, known as the Youth
Opportunities Programme, was modelled on the
Working Party's report, and some detailed suggestions, like the level of remuneration were
followed. It was intended that all young people
aged 16-18 who had been unemployed for at least 6
weeks should be eligible and that every school
leaver who failed to find employment should be
offered a place on the programme within a year.
At the same time the Minister announced the
Government's acceptance of a proposal from the
Manpower Services Commission to devise new ways to
deal with the unemployed aged over 18. One such
way to provide up to 8,000 places for adults from
the unemployment register who would act as
instructors and supervisors on the Youth Opportunities Programme. A second, and more important
way, was through the introduction of a new
programme, the Special Temporary Employment
Programme. This programme was to provide
temporary jobs for up to a year for people in the
age group 19 to 24, and for people aged 25 and
over who had been unemployed for more than a
year. Anyone engaged on the programme was to be
paid "the rate for the job" rather than an
allowance and it was estimated that the total
gross cost, assuming 25,000 places would be
provided, would be £68 million a year (the net
cost would be only about one third of this
figure). It was also stated that places on the
Special Temporary Employment Programme would be

concentrated in areas worst affected by the recession. One important provision for both the Youth Opportunities and the Special Temporary Employment Programmes was that they were given a degree of permanence in that the Government guaranteed to fund them for at least 5 years.

Both of the new programmes were to be administered through a new administrative structure. Although the Manpower Services Commission retained overall responsibility, it set up a new national body, the Special Programmes Board to direct the measures and at the local level 28 area boards were to be established, each consisting of representatives of trade unions, employers, local authorities, the education service, voluntary organisations and district manpower committees, to run the programmes

There were clear similarities between the Youth Opportunities Programme and the Special Temporary Employment Programme on the one hand and the Job Creation Programme and the Work Experience Programme on the other. The Youth Opportunities Programme was closest to the Work Experience Programme, not only because they both dealt with the 16-18 age group and paid participants an allowance rather than 'the wage for the job' but also because of similarities between the two programmes in the kind of tasks undertaken and experiences offered. The Special Temporary Employment Programme was closest to the Job Creation Programme, again because of the similarity of the age range covered, the kind of remuneration (a wage rather than an allowance) and the kind of tasks undertaken. In fact, on the introduction of the Special Temporary Employment Programme the Government made it clear that it hoped that Job Creation sponsors would continue with the new programme and suggested that they might like to transfer some projects to it. Of course there were some differences between the new and old programmes: for example, there was a clearer delineation of different types of experience and training in the Youth Opportunities Programme and a relaxation of the project criteria in the Special Temporary Employment Programme. Nevertheless, these differences being noted, the links between the old and the new programmes were clear and important.

In the first year of operation, 1978-79, both the Youth Opportunities and the Special Temporary

Employment Programme failed to reach their target intakes and the latter programme was also hit by Government financial restrictions: these meant that its budget allocation was cut by half. In 1979-80 the Special Temporary Employment Programme only offered places to about 22,000 (as against an initial target figure of over 35,000). However, the Youth Opportunities Programme was exempt from financial restrictions and managed to provide jobs for about 216,000 young people in 1979-80 (close to the initial target figure).

The information available about the way the Youth Opportunities Programme operated shows how priorities were ordered. Table 4.3 shows that by far the most popular branch of the Youth Opportunities Programme was that offering work experience on employers' premises: in 1979-80 this accounted for over 64 per cent of the total number of places offered on the Programme and over 76 per cent of all work experience places. Together the four work experience branches offered 84 per cent of all places on the Programme. It is also worthwhile noting that on average work experience places lasted for over twice as long as the work preparation courses. Most of the Youth Opportunity Programme places were provided by private sector sponsors (63 per cent in 1979-80): a significant proportion were provided by local authorities and other public bodies (26 per cent in 1979-80) with the balance being made up almost entirely by voluntary and charitable organisations (the Manpower Services Commission only provided about 1 per cent of all places itself). The private sector was a particularly important sponsor for work experience courses: in 1979-80 85 per cent of all work experience courses on employers premises were provided by private industry.

As far as the participants themselves are concerned, the majority of those on the Youth Opportunities Programme were 16 or 17 years old (in 1979-80 only 9 per cent were 18 years old). The participants were just about equally divided between girls and boys, although in some parts of the programme the balance was different (Training Workshops attracted more boys and Community Service more girls). Most participants who entered the Programme were current school leavers (for example 60 per cent of 1979-80 entrants left

Table 4.3: Youth Opportunities Programme 1979-80 Distribution of Entrants by Scheme Type

Scheme Type	No	%
Work Experience on Employers' Premises	138,900	64.2
Project Based Work Experience	15,200	7.0
Training Workshop	7,300	3.4
Community Service	20,700	9.6
Total Work Experience	182,100	84.2
Employment Industion Course	3,000	1.4
Short Training Courses	29,300	13.5
Remedial Courses	2,000	0.9
Total Work Preparation	34,300	15.8
Total all YOP	216,400	100.0

Source: Manpower Services Commission, Review of Second Year of Special Programme, p 11.

school between 1 August 1979 and 31 July 1979).

The Special Temporary Programme, as would be expected from the aims and provisions of the Programme, offered something of a contrast. All participants were over 18 years old, whereas all participants, apart from supervisors, in the Youth Opportunities programme were younger than this. However, it might be noted that the Special Temporary Employment Programme still did not match the objectives originally set out for it. In the original objectives it had been expected that most participants would come from the priority groups: these were those in the 19 and 24 age group who had been unemployed for more than 6 months and those over 25 who had been unemployed for more than a year. Table 4.4 shows that in practice in its second year of operation only 58 per cent of participants came from this group. The majority of participants in the Special Temporary Employment Programme were male (about 80 per cent, compared to the equal split in the Youth Opportunities Programme). Again the majority of places in the Special Temporary Employment Programme, unlike the majority of those in the Youth Opportunity Programme, were provided by local authorities (about a half) and voluntary organisations (about a third): in 1978-9 only 100 projects were sponsored by private industry and in the following year only 60 (this might be compared to the 500 projects provided in the Job Creation Programme in the last year of its operation, 1977-8).

Shortly before the end of 1980 the Government announced a number of changes to the then existing job creation programmes, changes which came into effect in the following year. Modifications were made to the Youth Opportunities Programme. Some involved the size and scope of the Programme: there was to be a 50 per cent increase in the number of places available (440,000 in 1981-2 compared to an increased target of 300,000 in 1980-1), an increase in the budget allocated to the Programme from £183 million in 1980-1 to £271 million in 1981-2, and a relaxation of the criteria governing precisely which 16 and 17 year olds were to be offered places on the Programme. Other changes related to the training content: following the evaluation of a pilot unified vocational preparation project it was decided to move towards a comprehensive system of vocational

Table 4.4: Characteristics of Entrants to the Special Temporary Employment Programme 1979-80

	1st Quarter	2nd Quarter	3rd Quarter	4th Quarter	Total
Total Number of Entrants	8,700	6,200	3,600	3,900	22,400
	%	%	%	%	%
Percentage of total were:					
Male	81	78	79	82	80
Female	19	22	21	18	20
Ages 19-24	47	50	52	54	50
Aged 25 and over	53	50	48	46	50
In the priority groups:					
Aged 19-24/over 6 months unemployed	29	35	39	45	34
Aged 25 and over/25 months unemployed	18	26	28	30	24
Total Priority Groups	47	61	67	75	58

Source: Manpower Services Commission, Review of Second Year of Special Programme, p 16.

preparation for all 16 and 17 year olds. This system was to be designed to provide basic work skills and personal advice and was to be linked to "off-the-job" training and further education.

More radical changes were announced as far as the Special Temporary Employment Programme was concerned. The Programme was to be replaced by a new Community Enterprise Programme. The new Programme was to be considerably larger than the old one: it was planned to provide 25,000 jobs (more than double the number in the old programme) and given a budget of £88 million for 1981-82 and £122 million in each of the two subsequent years (compared to an actual expenditure of £45 million on the Special Temporary Employment Programme in 1980-81). The Community Enterprise Programme also was to cover a larger geographical area than its predecessor in that it was not to be restricted to areas of highest unemployment.

Apart from coverage there were to be three other main differences between the Community Enterprise Programme and the Special Temporary Employment Programme. The first was that greater emphasis was to be placed on the need for projects to benefit local communities. Any such work was to be considered providing it was work which would not otherwise have been done within two years, and providing the appropriate trade unions supported it. The second was that additional emphasis was to be placed on training. For example, the project sponsors were to be reimbursed for the cost of off-the-job training and further education. The third was that increased efforts were to be made to attract sponsorship of projects from private firms and nationalised industries and funds were to be made available for partnerships in the creation of new enterprises between the public and private sectors.

Many of the other details of the Programme were similar to those of the Special Temporary Employment Programme. The administration of the Programme continued to be based on the Manpower Services Commission's Special Programme Division, Area Offices and Area Boards. The Programmes target groups were those in the age range 18 to 24 who had been unemployed for more than 6 months (the inclusion of 18 year olds was a change) and those over 25 years old who had been unemployed for more than one year, and participants were paid a wage based on "rate for the job" (subject to a maximum).

In some ways the changes that were made to the British job creation programmes in 1981 indicated a move back towards the way the programmes operated prior to 1978. In particular, the Community Enterprise Programme by stressing that the project undertaken must be of value to the local community was moving back towards the thinking behind the Job Creation Programme. Of course, not all the changes were in this direction. For example, the Community Enterprise Programme placed more emphasis on training than the Job Creation Programme. In practice the new job creation programmes were a mix of elements of the previous ones rather than a major new departure.

A major break was to be made, though, within the next two years as far as the youngest age range was concerned. At the end of 1981 discussions were started on a new training initiative. The initiative itself will be discussed in the next section. However, it can be noted that it represented an important change in emphasis in the approach of the Government to the problems of youth unemployment. The measure has a much clearer training objective than either the Youth Opportunities or the Work Experience Programme. Of course those initiatives made provision for training, but they retained an element of job creation as well.

The training initiative as a whole was not restricted to young people but its most important element, the Youth Training Scheme was: as far as over 18s were concerned the emphasis on job creation remained. A new job creation measure was announced to cover such people by the Chancellor of the Exchequer in his budget speech in March 1982. It was called the Community Programme and intended to provide 100,000 places. In his announcement the Chancellor of the Exchequer gave an indication of the thinking behind the Scheme.

> The central idea would be to give those who have been on the unemployment register for some time the chance to work for the benefit of their community, while still getting broadly the equivalent of their benefit entitlement plus an addition for expense and the like. They would remain free to take a regular job if it came

along. And it would be for them to decide whether or not to participate in such a scheme.

This concept may be unorthodox. Certainly it is no substitute for long-term jobs. But in today's world it makes a great deal of practical sense. The Government would like to see it tried, to see it carried through successfully, on a wide, indeed on a nationwide scale, with people working on non-profit making projects brought forward by local sponsors of all kinds, including voluntary organisations and the churches, and indeed local authorities[5].

In practice, of course, the programme has much in common with the Community Enterprise Programme. One commentator noted that the

reaction of those who had been working with the long-term unemployed through the Community Enterprise Programme (CEP) was one of pure amazement. That project exists to provide temporary jobs in projects of benefit to the community for the long-term unemployed. The Government appear to have re-invented the CEP.

One important difference between the Community Enterprise Programme and the Community Programme, though, is that the latter offers a lower level of renumeration to the participants: the Chancellor of the Exchequer talked about a rate similar to benefit entitlement, not the "rate for the job", subject to a maximum, as offered by the Community Enterprise Programme.

Training

Governments of all political complexions have supported the idea of industrial training for many years. Probably the most important development was the introduction of training boards in the 1960s. However, a number of important developments took place in the 1970s (such as, the setting up of the Training Opportunities Scheme) and this programme received a major boost in 1976 when the Training Services Agency was allocated a further £55 million to provide up to 35,000 extra training places. In the early 1980s further attention was given to training. A series of pilot projects on vocational training were introduced and in 1981 a number of measures designed to meet particular training needs were announced. £20 million was set aside for longer term skill training for young people and special measures were introduced linked to information technology. The most important development, though, occured later with the proposals for a comprehensive youth training initiative.

At the end of 1981 the Government published a White Paper on industrial training[7]. This White Paper followed a consultative document published by the Manpower Services Commission earlier that year. The White Paper, like the consultative document, was not simply concerned with training for unemployed young people: a number of more generally applicable measures were suggested, including, the development of an "Open Tech" programme to make technical training more accessible to those with the necessary ability. However, by far the most important proposal was specifically directed at the unemployed young: this was the introduction of a new Youth Training Scheme.

The White Paper proposed that all young people who left school at the minimum school leaving age and were unable to find work should be offered a place on the Youth Training Scheme: places should also be available, though not guaranteed, for other unemployed young people under 18 years of age. The aim of the scheme, was stated to be 'to equip unemployed young people to adapt successfully to the demands of employment; to have a fuller apreciation of the world of industry, business and technology in which they are working; and to develop basic and recognised skills which employers will require in the future'[8]. The intention was that these aims should be realised through planned and supervised work experience linked to off-the-job training or further education.

The White Paper's proposals were discussed in detail by the Manpower Services Commission, who set up a special Task Group to co-ordinate a response. Considerable controversy surrounded aspects of the Governments proposals, especially those concerning the level of payment and the withdrawal of Supplementary Benefit payments from

young people who did not "volunteer" to join the
scheme. This controversy was reflected in the
discussions in the MSC's Task Group. The Government had proposed that for those unemployed in
their first year after leaving school at the
minimum age the allowance should be set at a level
merely intended to cover travel and other expenses
(likely to be around £750 a year when the scheme
was to be introduced in 1983). The Government
also had proposed that young people who refused a
training place should not be entitled to Supplementary Benefit. In practice the Task Group did
not support the Government's recommendations on
either of these matters.

The Manpower Services Commission published its
detailed proposals for the Youth Training Initiative in the Spring of 1982. They suggested that
training schemes should last for a year and could
be run by a variety of different types of sponsor,
including private employers, voluntary organisations and local authorities. Sponsors could act
as managing agencies or could act through a
separate managing agency. It was proposed to pay
a fee of £1,850 per trainee to sponsors, and an
additional agency fee of £100. The scheme as a
whole was to be run by a National Supervisory
Board (replacing the existing Special Programmes
Board) though the detailed operation of the scheme
would be supervised by fifty to sixty local boards
who would keep a list of approved sponsors and
managing agencies.

The Government decided to accept the MSC's
proposals and this acceptance was announced by the
Summer of 1982. It was argued that acceptance had
been possible because employers would have to
share in the training costs, with the result that
the net cost of the scheme would be no greater
than that originally proposed by the government.
However, on the issue of the withdrawal of Supplementary Benefit for those school leavers refusing
to take part in the scheme the concession was less
than whole-heartedly given. Employment Secretary,
Norman Tebbit said on announcing his decision:

... The Government has noted the firmly
held and clearly expressed views of those
on who the operation of the scheme depends,
that its launch could be seriously impaired
by the withdrawal of Supplementary Benefit
from 16 year olds. We have therefore

decided that withdrawal of Supplementary
Benefit will not take place in September
1983 and that there will be a further
review after a year's operation of the
scheme[8].

However, the Government stated its intention
of retaining the provision that young people who
"unreasonably refused" a suitable offer of training would have their Supplementary Benefit reduced
for six weeks.

The new Youth Training Scheme was approved for
introduction in the Autumn of 1983. Initially, it
was to run alongside the Youth Opportunities
Programme, taking over some of its training
places, though later it superceded it completely.

Of course, industrial training and vocational
training can be justified in a period of low
unemployment. In fact, it is arguable that it is
likely to be most effective in such situations.
Training then, from this perspective, need not be
seen as a measure designed to deal with high
overall or high youth unemployment. However,
training also removes people from the active
labour force, even if only for a short period. As
such it might be attractive to governments to
expand training during periods of high unemployment to ease pressure on the labour market. It is
not intended at this stage to debate the extent to
which the Youth Training Scheme or any of the
earlier training measures was designed exclusively
with this purpose in mind. Nevertheless, there is
little doubt that such issues at least played a
role.

Measure to Reduce the Size of the Active Labour Force

The size of the active labour force can be affected by a variety of different factors, apart from
training. Of these, the attempts to persuade
workers to retire early have been the most important.

There is now a considerable body of evidence
which shows that in Britain economic activity
rates have fallen substantially in recent years
amongst the older sections of the population. For
example, between 1975 and 1982 economic activity
rates for males aged 60 to 64 fell from 84 to 64
per cent. Although not all of this reduction in

economic activity rates needs to be the result of early retirement there is other evidence[10] which suggests that a substantial proportion of it can be explained in this way.   Early retirement itself has been encouraged by the Government by a special policy measure and by a more general encouragement to moves in this direction.

The policy measure involved is the Job Release Scheme.   This was introduced in January 1977, and at that time it allowed men and women (working or unemployed but looking for work) in assisted areas to be paid a special tax free benefit (£23 a week) if they permanently left the labour market a year before the statutory pensionable age.   It was also made a condition of the scheme that the employer of anyone applying to join the scheme had to agree to recruit someone from the unemployment register as a replacement, although internal transfers to fill the particular job vacated were permitted providing someone else was recruited to fill the subsequent vacancy.

Since its introduction in 1977 a number of changes have been made to the detailed operation of the scheme.   For example, the ages covered have been changed a number of times: between March 1979 and March 1980 applications were sought from men aged 62 and 63 and disabled men over 60 as well as from men and women within one year of statutory pensionable age, but from April 1980 to November 1981 able-bodied men aged 62 and 63 were no longer allowed to apply, though these categories were again brought within the scope of the scheme from November 1981 and February 1982 (able-bodied men aged 63 were covered from November 1981 and those aged 62 from February 1982).   In November 1983 it was announced that able-bodied men aged 62 and 63 would again not be able to join the scheme from April 1984.   Similarly, the geographical coverage of the scheme was extended in 1978 (applications were sought from the whole of great Britain, not just assisted areas).   The provision allowing those unemployed but seeking work to apply was withdrawn in the middle of 1977, and the "replacement condition" was relaxed for a while for parts of the public sector (for instance, the Civil Service was allowed to recruit a replacement who was not on the unemployment register because of the policy of open competition operated for vacancies - this concession was withdrawn from April 1982).   Signi-

ficant changes also took place to the level and
make-up of the allowance paid. The value of the
allowance had been raised to £57.35 a week by 1983
and a higher rate of allowance (at the same time
as the figure previously quoted, £70.55 a week)
was paid to those with dependents but without
significant earnings themselves. A version of the
scheme has now been introduced for part-time
employees.

The number of people joining the scheme in the
early years was relatively small. For example, by
mid-1978 about 24,000 people had joined the
scheme, out of which just over half had been
employed immediately before. However, in later
years the numbers joining the scheme increased
markedly. The reduction of the age limits in 1981
and 1982 gave an important boost. In 1982/83
46,852 males joined the scheme and by June 1983
the total number of males attracted to it since
its introduction had risen to 195,288.

The encouragement given by the Government to
early retirement in other ways is more difficult
to pin down and to document. However, in many
ways, it has probably been more important. It has
been effective, in part, as a result of the
Government's own actions as a major employer, and
in part as the result of the more general encouragement the Government has given to others to
follow this lead. Most public sector employees
are members of an occupational pension scheme.
Over 90 per cent of workers in nationalised
industries are now members of occupational pension
schemes; over 80 per cent of workers in other
public corporations and almost all workers in
central government are members. Most of the
public sector schemes allow members to take
enhanced pensions on early retirement and in a
number of areas, such as the coal mining industry,
the steel industry, the civil service, local
authorities and education, special early retirement schemes have been introduced. In many public
sector industries substantial numbers of employees
have been encouraged by these provisions to accept
early retirement. A lower proportion of employees
in the private sector are members of occupational
pension schemes, but the proportion has been
growing in recent years and in many cases the
provisions that have been introduced in the public
sector to encourage early retirement have been
followed in the private sector.

It is clear that in many cases early retirement while it leads to a reduction in the size of the active labour force does not lead to a direct reduction in the numbers unemployed, for not all those who leave jobs are replaced. The effectiveness of early retirement schemes as a way of dealing with high levels of unemployment is a subject for separate examination. Nevertheless, it is clear that this has been one of the main policy objectives of early retirement.

Early retirement aside, a number of other ways of reducing the active labour force have been suggested. Measures to encourage young people to stay on at school after the statutory minimum school leaving age (such as the £60 million announced for this purpose in 1981), like training, can be justified on a variety of grounds, not simply as a way of reducing the size of the active labour force, though there is little doubt that this latter consideration has been important. Some of the other suggestions, like increased recruitment into the armed forces, have received widespread discussion but little direct policy attention as yet[10].

Conclusions

A wide range of special employment measures have been introduced, then, in Britain in the 1970s and early 1980s with the aim of alleviating the worst effects of youth unemployment. The nature and detailed provisions of such measures has changed rapidly. This can most clearly be seen in the type of job creation measures used. The first major job creation measure, the Job Creation Programme was introduced in 1975 while the Work Experience Programme was introduced in 1976. They were re-placed in 1978 by the Special Temporary Employment Programme and the Youth Opportunities Programme. The first of these programmes was itself replaced in 1981 by the Community Enterprise Programme and then the Community Programme while the Youth Opportunities Programme was phased out in 1983 to make way for the Youth Training Scheme. Nevertheless, the central aim has been the same throughout: to try to fid ways to reduce the level of youth unemployment without having major effects on net public expenditure and the rate of inflation. One of he most important questions to be asked is whether such measures can

succeed on their own terms and whether youth
unemployment can be tackled by policies that have
such a specific focus.

Before dealing with this specific question we
turn to look at some of the motives behind the
introduction of the policies reviewed. Essentially the concern is with the policy debate
though in the course of reviewing this debate the
issues about the social consquences of youth
unemployment highlighted in Chapter 1 will be
raised again.

Notes

1. National Management Board, 17315.
2. Manpower Services Commission, Young People and
    Work, 1977.
3. Joint Memorandum by the Department of Employ-
    ment and Manpower Services Commission to House
    of Commons Expediture Committee,
    9 February 1977, Annex A.
4. Manpower Services Commission, Op Cit, p 29.
5. Sir Geoffrey Howe, March 9th, 1982 House of
    Commons.
6. Unemployment Bulletin, April 1982, p 3.
7. Department of Employment, A New Training
    Initiative: A Programme for Action, HMSO,
    London, 1981 Cmnd 8455.
8. Ibid p 7.
9. Department of Employment Gazette, July 1982, p
    278.
10. Evidence from the General Household Survey
    shows that betwen 1975 and 1977 the percentage
    of males aged 60 to 64 claiming to be economi-
    cally inactive because of retirement rose from
    4.5 per cent to 7.8 per cent.
11. A scheme for young people to spend 2 to 3
    weeks in the armed forces was announced in
    1982 though this was not linked to unemploy-
    ment as earlier suggestions had argued it
    should be. In 1983 an Armed Forces version of
    the Youth Training Scheme was introduced.

Chapter Five

THE POLITICAL DEBATE

In the first chapter a number of the reasons why
youth unemployment has been seen as a cause for
concern were reviewed. The approach was a fairly
general one centring on research evidence. In
this chapter the focus is somewhat narrower, on
the political discussion that has formed the
background to the policy initiatives on youth
unemployment. In essence, then, the question
addressed in this chapter is: what rationale has
been put forward in the political debates for the
policy approaches adopted?

It is important to stress that the aim is to
review the political debate rather than to present
a complete analysis of the factors influencing
policy making. An analysis of policy making would
demand much more detailed discussion of the
origins and pressures for policy options. Clearly
it would need to range wider than simply the
political discussion and to encompass, for
example, the impact of policy advice from the
civil service. The aim here, then, is much more
limited and focused on public discussion of the
policy.

Concern for the Unemployed

There is a long tradition of writers viewing the
development of social policy as a response to the
compassion felt for the 'less fortunate' members
of society by those who are influential in such
matters[1]. In the case of the development of the
welfare state in Britain it has been argued that
expansion of services has been a response to
pressure from a number of people and groups, often
moved by religious conviction, who felt that the

extent of the inequalities in society was unacceptable. Particular concern was felt for
vulnerable groups like the disabled and children,
and frequently initial provision was made just for
such groups, but eventually spread to other
sections of society. A similar line of argument
can be pursued in the case of recent policies
designed to deal with the worst problems arising
from youth unemployment, for there is no doubt
that many politicians and others who are influential in policy making have felt compassion for the
young unemployed. Politicians, from all political
parties have expressed such feelings publicly on
many occasions. For example, in a debate in the
House of Commons in March 1982 Members of Parliament from all political parties showed that they
were aware of the misery of youth unemployment and
that they were concerned that something should be
done to alleviate it. A recurring theme was that
unemployment statistics by themselves could not
properly convey the misery they reflected. Thus
one member said in the debate:

> I can give the House figures. All hon-
> members can bandy the figures about, but
> each person on the dole is a personal human
> tragedy, not a statistic. Families face
> deprivation and their standards of living
> are cut. In my young day the problem was
> whether the kids had shoes. Today, the
> problem is whether, when the kids go to
> school, they are comparable with their
> classmates in what they talk about and do.
> Personal tragedies cannot be expressed in
> statistics. In the last three years at my
> Saturday surgery I have watched heartbreak
> after heartbreak. We can offer no
> immediate comfort[2].

These views were echoed in a later speech
which again stressed the inability of statistics
to convey the full extent of the problem.

> The hon-member for Brent, South (Mr Pavitt)
> is right to say that we should not think in
> terms of statistics. We are talking about
> human hardship and people who are suffering
> and whose families are experiencing grave
> problems[3].

The Political Debate

It is important also to stress that such expressions of concern have not been restricted to back bench Members of Parliament. Thus, Sir Geoffrey Howe in his budget speech in 1982 said:

> To have millions of people at a time without work, many of them for long periods, is a tragic loss to any community. To be unable to find work is an affront to personal self-respect[4].

In fact, the Chancellor went on in this same budget speech to state that because there was such concern for the plight of the unemployed he intended to introduce a new special employment measure, the Community Programme.

It is important, though, to recognise the status of such comments. They are an expression of concern, and no doubt concern genuinely felt. In the case of the concern expressed by the Chancellor of the Exchequer they are an indication of the views held by somebody closely involved in policy making and were linked directly to a policy initiative. However, they are only a small part of the public debate. The concern expressed over the consequences of youth unemployment for society as a whole has been just, if not more important.

Social Control

One of the strongest challenges to the view that social policy has developed primarily as a result of the compassion felt by policy makers has come from writers who have presented a radical critique of social policy. For example, what have sometimes been called 'social control theories' of social policy,[5] have suggested that social policies have been used as a way of controlling social unrest, either by removing the principle focus of such unrest (but leaving the underlying causes untouched) or by using the threat of the withdrawal of social service benefit as a means of disciplining the workforce and encouraging the development of desirable attitudes. The crucial assumption behind such theories is that those in power believe that there is a threat of social unrest and believe that the development of certain types of social policy will help to remove it; whether or not either belief is correct may be unimportant, for action will be taken by policy

makers on the basis of what they perceive the
position to be, rather than on the basis of what
an outside observer may assess.

In the case of special employment measures for
the young there is a good deal of evidence from
the public debate to support such a point of
view. There is little doubt, for example, that
many public figures were concerned about the
threat of social unrest, and that this fear was
heightened by the riots in many British cities in
1981. The report into the riots by Lord Scarman
itself drew attention to the link between social
unrest and youth unemployment. It was pointed out
that high levels of youth unemployment, allied to
other social deprivations, were an important part
of the cause of the riots, though Lord Scarman was
quick to argue also that the social conditions did
not excuse the riots.

> The social conditions in Brixton - many of
> which are to be found in other inner city
> areas - do not provide an excuse for dis-
> order. They cannot justify attacks on the
> police in the streets, arson or riot. All
> of those who in the course of the disorders
> in Brixton and elsewhere engaged in vio-
> lence against the police were guilty of
> grave criminal offences, which society, if
> it is to survive, cannot condone... At the
> same time, the disorders in Brixton cannot
> be fully understood unless they are seen in
> the context of the complex political,
> social and economic factors to which I have
> briefly referred. In analysing communal
> disturbances such as those in Brixton and
> elsewhere, to ignore the existence of these
> factors is to put the nation in peril[6].

The last part of this quotation shows that
Lord Scarman did not only link unemployment to
social disorder, but also that he argued it was
such an important cause of social disorder that if
it was ignored the stability of society would be
imperilled. Two further quotations show how this
argument recurred and was expanded upon later in
the report. The first quotation is interesting
because it starts with a comment on special
employment measures, and is followed by a note on
the need to deal with the long-term problem of
unemployment if social stability is to be secured.

... Government - in the shape of the Department of Employment and the Manpower Services Commission (MSC) - is clearly already doing much to try to alleviate the worst effects of unemployment, particularly among the young. The effectiveness of those programmes, and the broad thrust of economic policy, lie outside the scope of my Inquiry. I therefore simply note the criticisms made to me of the MSC programmes that they do not prepare young people sufficiently well for skilled work, and that they do not cater adequately for ethnic minority needs. Both the nature of the training provision to be made for the young unemployed and the wider economic issues are already the subject of vigorous national debate: it is unnecessary for me to comment on them.

I do, however, offer one thought for consideration in that debate. The structural causes of unemployment - which include remarkable developments in technology, an effect of which is that leading developed countries are losing the attributes of a labour intensive economy - are deeper and more complex than the mere existence of the current recession. If this analysis is right, we shall have to face its implications. In order to secure social stability, there will be a long-term need to provide useful, gainful employment and suitable educational, recreational and leisure opportunities for young people, especially in the inner city[7].

The second quotation is taken from the last substantive paragraph of the report. In it Lord Scarman draws an analogy between the civil disorders in the USA in the 1960s and the British riots of 1981, quoting President Johnson to stress again the link between social conditions and social stability. Interestingly the quotation shows that President Johnson was concerned to be able to answer the accusation that he was not motivated simply by fear of conflict, by stating that he was fired by compassion, though, nevertheless, he drew attention to the dangers of failing to take action to remedy the problems.

I end with the quotation from President
Johnson's address to the nation which appeared
at the very beginning of the US Report of the
National Advisory Commission on Civil
Disorders (1968):-

"... The only genuine, long range solution for
what has happened lies in an attack - mounted
at every level - upon the conditions that
breed despair and violence. All of us know
what those conditions are: ignorance, discrimination, slums, poverty, disease, not
enough jobs. We should attack these
conditions - not because we are frightened by
conflict, but because we are fired by con-
science. We should attack them because there
is simply no other way to achieve a decent and
orderly society in America ..."

These words are as true of Britain today as
they have been proved by subsequent events to
be true of America[8].

In the debate in the House of Commons that
followed the publication of the Scarman report
many Members of Parliament echoed Lord Scarman's
remarks about the link between youth unemployment
and social unrest. Thus, one member argued that,

... while relations with the police are a
crucial factor, if I had to rate the causes
of what happened in order of importance,
unemployment would rank second. The
figures are extremely high. They had
increased dramatically before the riots,
and they have increased dramatically
since. What worries me, however, is that
unemployment so corrodes the attitudes of
young people in particular that when the
level of unemployment falls there may be no
corresponding fall in crime and social
behaviour[9].

A similar comment was made by another con-
tributor to the same debate who suggested a direct
link between the unemployment problems of school
leavers and riots.

Lord Scarman writes not only about the
police, but about the economic conditions

found in city areas. He points out that unemployment, overcrowding and a lack of recreational facilities are not an excuse for crime. However, no Hon Member would deny that the possibility of further outbreaks of violence has increased, because the number of unemployed youngsters in Lambeth today is 62 per cent higher than it was a year ago and 40 per cent higher than it was a few months ago, when the riots broke out.

It is no coincidence that the first outbreak of violence in 1980 and 1981, in Bristol and Brixton, took place in April, in the week before Easter, at the end of the spring term, as the first crop of the year's school leavers found themselves outside their classrooms and on the dole queue. We must consider what we are offering the "class of 82".

Concern about the need to deal with the underlying causes of social unrest has been matched by concern about the effects of prolonged unemployment on the attitudes of young people, particularly on attitudes towards work. One Member of Parliament, John Fraser, commented on the way in which unemployment can undermine the willingness of young people to strive to prepare themselves better for the world of work.

Unemployment also leads to the loss of any kind of moral sanction. One used to be able to tell people that if they worked hard, gained educational qualifications and were prompt in their attendance at work, the rewards would come. But people no longer believe that, because even the highly qualified find it difficult to obtain a job. Therefore, disillusion creeps in. It even creeps into the schools, because there, too, it is widely believed that even if a pupil achieves something in his final years it will be of no use to him when he leaves. I do not endorse that attitude, but it is understandable that the corrosiveness creeps back into the educational system[11].

Jim Prior, when Secretary of state for Employment similarly warned of the danger that prolonged experience of unemployment would erode the "ability to work".

> The long-term unemployed after a prolonged period of time are damaged by the psychological element attached to all this and it makes it much harder for them ever to pick up work again[12].

In this way, then, it can be argued that long-term unemployment can pose a danger to social stability of a rather different kind. The danger is posed not by the immediate threat of social unrest but by the change in attitudes which may mean that young people no longer fit easily into the work roles that society may require at least some of them to fulfil.

Such evidence clearly supports the view that one of the factors in the minds of policy makers when proposing special employment measures has been social control. However, it is important to recognise that contrary voices have been heard: for example, the view has been expressed that Members of Parliament, as well as other commentators, have paid too much attention to the extent to which high levels of unemployment might lead to a challenge to social stability. For instance, in the debate on the Scarman report one Member of Parliament broke away from the general view that the underlying causes of social unrest had been correctly identified and argued that the report paid too much attention to social conditions and too little directly to "law and order".

> Lord Scarman I am sure has produced a good report on the facts but in his conclusion and judgements he was actuated too much by political considerations. After all, he is one of our most politically conscious judges, and for that reason his judgement was faulty.

> The report is flawed and it is not of as much assistance to us in forming our future policies as most Hom Members seem to believe. The question is essentially about the maintenance of law and order[13].

Further, it was not just back bench Conservative Members of Parliament who expressed such
views. On the day that the Scarman inquiry was
established the Prime Minister appeared on tele-
vision and declared that the level of unemployment
had not been a major factor in the riots.

More generally, critics of social control
theories of social policy have argued that such
theories do not take into account sufficiently the
influence of the "anti-welfare" lobby[14]. Such a
lobby does not accept the view that social
stability is threatened by inadequate social
policy provision; to the contrary, it takes the
view that such provision itself can weaken
society, reduce incentives to work and enterprise. The scepticism expressed on the extent to
which high levels of unemployment can be seen as a
"cause" of the 1981 riots does not follow the line
of argument of the anti-welfare lobby through
fully but it is certainly consistent with it, and
many of the politicians who expressed such opinions, if comments on other matters are taken into
account, can be categorised as members of the
"anti-welfare" lobby

If we are to take notice of this "anti-
welfare" lobby and to view it as at least a
partial challenge to the social control theory of
social policy then we need to explain why, in
spite of such views, some of the politicians
referred to, at the end of the day, accepted the
introduction of special employment measures. In
practice the explanation may lie in the consideration of more detailed party political issues.

Party Political Considerations

Youth unemployment has been a matter that has
attracted a good deal of attention not just from
Members of Parliament but also from the media,
from prominent organisations, like trade unions,
and from all the indications available, from the
public in general. In such a situation it should
not be surprising if politicians have felt themselves to be under some pressure to show that they
have been doing all that they can to deal with the
problem. Such a view does not suggest that some
politicians, for other reasons would not have
wanted to take action to deal with high levels of
youth unemployment anyway: for them this would
simply have provided an additional incentive to

take action. Such a view, however, also provides
an explanation for the decision of politicians to
support action over youth unemployment when otherwise they might not have done so.

When the Labour Party came into power in 1974
it did so on the basis of an agreed programme with
the unions, initially referred to as the "social
compact" but later talked about as the "social
contract". The agreement ranged widely and can be
viewed as an important development both from the
point of view of the way that British trade unions
have sought to achieve their objectives and from
the point of view of social policy. In essence,
the trade unions were given an undertaking on a
variety of different policy matters in return for
an understanding on incomes. In the first year or
so of the life of the social contract the agreement seemed to have relatively little effect on
wage levels, though later the effect was much more
noticeable. As far as social policy is concerned
the effect of the social contract is debatable.
Some commentators[15] have argued that in practice
the trade unions gained very little from the
social contract that they would not have got
anyway, and that it did not prevent the Labour
Government embarking on public expenditure cuts
from 1976 until the end of their period of
office. Nevertheless, while the tangible benefits
for the unions may be debateable, it is clear that
the Government had to persuade the unions that it
was doing all it could to meet the agreed objectives. In other words it had to show that failure
to meet objectives was not the result of disagree-
ment over the objectives themselves; rather, it
was the result of developments (in particular, in
the world economy) outside national control. In
such circumstances it was extremely important that
the Government should be seen to be "doing what it
could" to deal with rising unemployment, even if
in practice it was unable to alter the situation
significantly. This is clear from the comments of
Michael Foot, then Secretary of State for Employment, in the House of Commons.

My Hon Friends asked, first, a question
about unemployment. I refer to that
because of the figures I gave the House
earlier and the statement made by others
that over the coming months we may have to

face figures that are even worse in some respects than those we have to face today.

I certainly do not minimise the significance of these dangers, in any sense. Of course, if unemployment were to soar upwards, it could do the greatest possible injury to the operation of the social contract, apart from any other objections that we would have to such a happening and all the human considerations that are involved.[16]

Later in the same debate Michael Foot made specific reference to the link between the special employment measures and discussion over the social contract.

As part of the social contract the Government will be considering the proposals which have been put forward by the Manpower Services Commission and other such bodies, because we see absolutely eye to eye with what Mr Len Murray said the other day, namely, that fighting against unemployment is also an essential part of the social contract itself[17].

It should be stressed that it is not suggested that the special employment measures introduced placated trade union anger at rising unemployment. Some trade union leaders argued for traditional demand management techniques to be used to alleviate the situation. However, while the government was unwilling to take such action, special employment measures represented a demonstration of concern and an indication of a willingness to take at least some action.

The position of the Conservative Government, from 1979, was somewhat different to that of its Labour predecessor. The Conservative Government was not as vulnerable to trade union pressure, and initially did not seem to be affected by pressure to take further action to halt the rise in the level of unemployment. In its first year, for example, the Conservative Government reduced support for a whole range of different special employment measures. Two reasons were given for this move. The first was that there was a need to reduce the level of public expenditure and the

changes made to the special employment measures
would result in a saving of £170 million. The
second was that the only way to deal with unemployment in the long term was to alter the general
economic climate. It was accepted that special
measures might have a role in the short-term but
there was scepticism about the extent of even the
short-term role they should have: in the case of
the Special Temporary Employment Programme it was
explicitly claimed that the measure was not being
targetted sufficiently on priority groups and that
its coverage had been extended too widely. The
thinking behind the Government's policy at this
time was made clear in the many public pronounce-
ments on the issue. For example, in a Parliamentary debate on unemployment the Government made
it clear that they believed that unemployment
would only be brought under control when general
economic conditions improved and in particular
when inflation was reduced. Thus, in the debate,
the Government tabled a motion that

> This House deeply regrets the high level of
> unemployment both here and in other parts
> of the world, but recognises that the
> conquest of inflation is a necessary
> precondition for the creation of new jobs
> in soundly based and competitive industry
> upon which a realistic solution to the
> problem depends[18].

In fact, even before they had won the election
and gained office the Conservative Party had made
it clear that this would be the line they would
pursue. Thus, in their election manifest they had
said:

> Too much emphasis has been placed on
> attempts to preserve existing jobs. We
> need to concentrate more on the creation of
> conditions in which new, more modern, more
> secure, better paid jobs come into exist-
> ence. This is the best way of helping the
> unemployed and those threatened with the
> loss of their jobs in the future[19].

There was also a view underlying this argument
that it was not the Government that was to blame
for the high level of unemployment, but individuals and groups like trade unions, and to an

extent the unemployed themselves. Individuals, and groups like the trade unions, were to blame because they had helped to "make Britain uncompetitive" by high wage claims and low productivity which were one of the important causes of inflation. The unemployed themselves were to blame because they were unwilling to accept certain jobs, they were not willing to move to find work, and they were not willing to work because they were "better off" relying on state financial aid. Two quotations from Conservative Members of Parliament can be used to illustrate such views. The first is from Dudley Smith, the Member of Parliament for Warwick and Leamington, in which he first proclaims his belief in the underlying philosophy of Government policy and then turns to some of the problems created by the inflexibility of unions, managements and the unemployed themselves.

I subscribe to the Governments basic policy. I believe it to be essential for our long-term economic recovery. No one has ever pretended that the way could be easy. Indeed, it was stressed that it would be painful ....

.... my right Hon Friend the Secretary of State put his finger right on the problem when he talked about the necessity for "real" jobs. Cosmetic exercises are no good. By all means let us take temporary measures, especially for young people. But, at the end of the day, unless we get right the infrastructure of our industry and economy and unless we get the kind of jobs which will last and provide people with lifelong employment, we shall decline very seriously as a nation ....

Many employees fail to display flexibility in modern conditions, in which they should display far less rigidity. Attitudes on both sides are often wrong and therefore partly responsible for todays situation ....

A different attitude is needed on the part of management and unions, and also probably by the individual as regards his working ability. The lush days of full employment, when it was easy to walk out of one job and into another, and to pick up reasonably good pay and to secure increases without any extra effort have gone forever. This is largely because of advancing technology, which will mean that there are fewer jobs available and far more competition for them.

In these circumstances the individual must be more flexible, he must be prepared to move to new employment, even if it is socially unpleasant for him to do so[20].

The second quotation is from Jim Prior when he was Secretary of State for Employment. In this quotation he stresses that the government cannot be blamed for everything and that the level of unemployment is just as much the responsibility of individuals.

.... I want to get this bit off my chest rather badly. Yesteray, on the programme "The World This Weekend", I said - and I repeat it now - that the Government cannot do everything. People have to do something for themselves. As a nation we have always liked to blame someone else. We blame the Government, we blame the management or we blame the unions. I think that we all have to take a share of the responsibility for what has happened in recent years [21].

This point of view does not suggest that all special employment measures should be scrapped immediately. However, it views them as being relatively unimportant as a long-term solution, and because of their public expenditure consequences, potentially even counter-productive in the long term. The practical implication of such views is likely to be, as it was in 1979, that special employment measures will be retained but at a reduced level.

However, although this point of view seemed to dominate the strategy of the Conservative Government in the first year or so of its office it was modified subsequently. Its modification did not appear to result from a change in underlying philosophy or approach: rather, it appeared as if the change was a reflection of two matters, one of which was the appreciation of the pressure and importance of public opinion on the matter. The Government came under increasing attack from the Labour Party for its "lack of concern" for the unemployed. Typical of such attacks was that made by Eric Varley, then opposition spokesman on employment

.... I know that unemployment is always an amusing subject for Conservative members. We can always guarantee a laugh from the Conservatives when we talk about unemployment. What is the result of this orchestrated effort? It is certainly impressive. It is the wanton destruction of hundreds and thousands of jobs. Self-respecting men and women are prevented from making their contribution to the well-being of the country[22].

Such charges were strenuously denied by Government spokesmen, yet there is little doubt that the attacks, and the degree of public support they seemed to attract (public opinion polls for example, showed that unemployment rather inflation had by this time become the main cause for general concern) worried the Government. The concern felt in Government circles about such accusations was expressed in a speech by Jim Prior in a debate in the House of Commons. Thus, he said,

.... the only point I make is that I do not think, at ths stage, with the record that the Labour Party had when in Government, that Labour members have any right to hawk their social consciences around the House this afternoon. The Right Hon Gentleman tries to make out that the Conservative members regard unemployment as a joke and that we laugh about it, but let me tell him that we in the Conservative Government have a better record on unemployment than the Labour Party has[24].

The argument, then, is that even those members of the Government that believed in a longer term approach to unemployment and doubted the value of special employment measures were persuaded to accept them, in part, because they were stung by the growing public accusation that they were not concerned about the level of unemployment. In this context it was important for the Government to be able to show, for party political reasons, that they were concerned about the level of unemployment and willing to take what action they could, even if they remained convinced that the longer term solution lay in another direction.

This point has been made in another context by Moon. He has pointed out that despite the opposition parties' success in raising the unemployment issue in the 1983 General Election campaign the Conservative vote declined by only 1.5 per cent and the Government increased its parliamentary majority. He argues that unemployment will remain the key political issue 'and the maintenance of the Government's standing will depend largely on its continuing to be seen to be "doing something" by way of special employment measures, and continuing to minimise the political symbolism of the numbers of people officially without work'[25]. A similar point has been made by Richardson and Henning when they discuss the policy responses of Western Governments as being 'either symbolic actions or placebos administered to the electorate'[26].

The second reason for the change in attitude towards special employment measures by some members of the Conservative Governments of the early 1980s was that such measures were seen to give them the opportunity to intervene in sections of education and training and alter the balance of provision. This issue is dealt with more fully in later chapters, though for the moment it is important to recall that the aim was to ensure that education and training became more relevant to the "needs of industry". Such a change had clear attractions to many members of the Government who had accepted an argument, which was by no means restricted to the ranks of the Conservative Party, that one of the reasons for Britain's poor economic performance was that there was too great a gap between education and training on the one hand and industry on the other.

Conclusion

It is clear, then, that a number of different points of view have been put forward in the political debate over policy making for youth unemployment. At times, concern for the plight of the unemployed has been stressed, at others fear of social unrest has been a central concern, and at still other times more detailed party political matters have seemed to dominate. It is important, though, that these views should not be presented simply as alternatives, for at times individuals and political parties have seemed to express support for more than one of them.

The policy on special employment measures has not been entirely consistent since the mid 1970s. As has already been noted, changes in emphasis have occurred, and for a while it appeared as though the last Conservative Government was moving to scale dowm initiatives in this area. However, despite such variations in approach, there has been a degree of continuity in the general orientation of policy despite changes in Government and despite changes in personnel with primary responsibility for this area.

It is arguable that one of the reasons for this general continuity has been that it has been possible to support the policy aproach from a number of different, and with a mixture of, objectives. Of course, alternative policy approaches exist to the one that has been adopted. Youth unemployment could have been tackled by the use of more traditional demand management techniques, or it could have been left on the assumption that young people like others will only be able to be offered "real" jobs once the economy as a whole has been placed on a "sounder footing". However, while both of these approaches have had their adherents neither has made a major impact on the British political scene since the mid 1970s. The latter came close to doing so in the late 1970s with the election of the first Thatcher Government, but that approach never fully gained sway in the case of youth unemployment and receded in the 1980s. Clearly politicians who were unwilling to take either of these policy approaches gravitated towards special employment measures as a valuable palliative if not long-term solution for youth unemployment.

Essentially, then, at least publically, politicians of all political parties have put forward a number of justifications for some action being taken to deal with youth unemployment. It is impossible from this review to judge private evaluations or motives. However, it would not be surprising if in private as well as in public the motives for supporting special employment measures were similarly complex and represented a coalition of different rather than one overriding interest.

In the next chapter we move on from looking at the debate that preceded the introduction of special employment measures to look at the impact of those directed at the young. To what extent have they achieved their explicit policy objectives and what other consequences of their operation should be highlighted?

Notes

1. In many ways this has been the dominant tradition in social policy though in recent years this tradition has been challenged. See, for example, R Mishra, Society and Social Policy: Theoretical Perspective on Welfare, Macmillan, London, 1981.
2. Hansard, 5 March, 1982, p 524.
3. Hansard, 5 March, 1982, p 524.
4. Hansard, 9 March, 1980, p 730.
5. See, J Higgins, 'Social Control Theories of Social Policy', Journal of Social Policy, Vol 9, No 11, 1980, pp 1-23.
6. Home Office, The Brixton Disorders 10-12 April, 1981: Report on an Inquiry by the Rt Hon Lord Scarman, OBE, HMSO, London, 1981, Cmnd 82, pp 14-15.
7. Ibid, pp 107-8.
8. Ibid, p 136.
9. Hansard, 10 December, 1981, pp 1042-3.
10. Hansard, 10 December, 1981, 1032.
11. Hansard, 10 December, 1981, p 1043.
12. Hansard, 14 July, 1980, p 1089.
13. Hansard, 10 December, 1981, p 1044.
14. See, for example, J Higgins, The Poverty Business: Britain and America, Basil Blackwell/Martin Robertson, Oxford, 1978.
15. R Taylor, Labour and the Social Contract, Fabian Tract, 458, Civil Press, Glasgow, 1978.
16. Hansard, 23 January, 1975, p 1805.
17. Hansard, 23 January, 1975, p 1806.
18. Hansard, 14 July, 1980, p 1081.
19. Quoted by E C Varley in the House of Commons. Reported in Hansard, 14 July, 1980, p 1070.
20. Hansard, 14 July, 1980, pp 1100-1.
21. Hansard, 14 July, 1980, pp 1086-7.
22. Hansard, 14 July, 1980, p 1073.
24. Hansard, 14 July, 1980, p 1084.

25. J Moon, "The Responses of British Governments to Unemployment" in J Richardon, R Henning, Unemployment: Policy Responses of Western Democracies, Sage, London, 1984, p 38.
26. J Richardson, R Henning, Ibid, p 315.

Chaper Six

THE IMPACT OF SPECIAL EMPLOYMENT MEASURES ON YOUTH UNEMPLOYMENT

In any review of special employment measures directed at the young it is important to look at the overall impact of such measures as well as at the detailed implications of individual instruments. However, for the moment it is the latter matter with which we are concerned. The intention then is to examine the main special employment measures directed at the young and to attempt an assessment of their operation. Initially, job creation and training will be considered, though later other items like subsidies, will be looked at and measures like early retirement, that clearly are not directed at the young but nevertheless might affect their employment chances.

Job Creation Programmes

Job creation programmes in Britain, and in most other countries, have had three central aims. The first has been temporarily to remove participants from the ranks of the unemployed, and in this way, to combat some of the undesirable consequences of unemployment. The second, has been to improve the chances of participants obtaining normal employment in the future. In essence it has been hoped that either because of the training offered on job creation programmes or simply because such programmes offer participants an opportunity to show that they are able to work effectively, when they leave programmes, participants will be able to compete better in the labour market. The third aim, has been to undertake tasks which produce a good or service of value to the community at large. It should be noted, though, that not all programmes have emphasised this last point. For

example, in Britain in the case of the Work
Experience Programme and the Youth Opportunities
Programme this was not suggested as a central
aim. It should also be noted that certain
programmes have put more emphasis on one of the
three aims than others. Again, both the Work
Experience Programme and the Youth Opportunities
Programme placed most emphasis on the aim of
improving participants' future chances in the
labour market as the result of the training
offered.

It can reasonably be claimed that job creation
programmes have had some success in meeting the
first of their aims in Britain. The number of
places offered on the programmes and therefore the
number of young people removed from the ranks of
the unemployed, has risen substantially since the
programmes were first introduced. The first major
programmes, Job Creation and Work Experience, at
maximum only offered 34,000 and 10,000 places at
any one time respectively, and in the case of the
Job Creation Programme by no means all of these
places were offered to young people. In 1982 the
Youth Opportunities Programme alone offered about
half a million places, and all of them were to 16
to 18 year olds.

The crude figures of participants, though, do
not necessarily show the full extent to which the
programmes have helped to take people off the
unemployment register, for job creation programmes
may lead to the opening of a variety of additional
employment opportunities, some of them long-term.
Some of the opportunities may be directly connected with the projects (such as those linked to
the supervision and administration of the programme); others may be connected to the product of
the projects (for instance, a job creation programme may be used to build amenities which will
need to be maintained by permanent emloyees after
the job creation work has been completed); others
may be only indirectly connected to job creation
projects (to the extent that job creation projects
result in participants obtaining a higher income
than would have been the case if they were out of
work – this might result in higher consumer expenditure which in turn might result in new employment opportunities). Estimates of the total
employment effect of job creation vary, and there
is evidence that certain kinds of projects tend to
lead to the opening of more opportunities addi-

tional to those available directly to participants than others. Nevertheless, there is no doubt that simply to examine the number of places directly created on projects alone will mean that part of the picture has been missed.

However, to balance this assessment it also needs to be taken into account that in some cases job creation openings may simply be a substitute for what otherwise would have been normal engagements: what is often referred to as the "displacement effect". Attempts have been made to guard against this: the rules governing project approval normally state that work cannot be undertaken which otherwise would have been done in the normal course of events and the involvement of trade unions in vetting is designed to ensure that this rule is adhered to. Official comments recognise that in Britain displacement does occur but suggest that it is a relatively minor problem. For example, a survey conducted in 1980 for the MSC has been used to suggest that displacement occurred in only 30 per cent of cases in the branch of the Youth Opportunities Programme looked at. However, it needs to be stressed that the figure quoted only referred to employers who admitted substituting YOP participants for other workers. Others may have practiced substitution but not admitted it. Studies of the displacement effect by international agencies, like the EEC, have suggested that it may be a problem particularly with larger projects and studies in the USA have suggested that the displacement effect can rise over the lifetime of a programme, and may reach as much as 50 per cent[1]. In practice it is impossible to give a precise figure for displacement and, as with additional employment, experience will vary from project to project. Nevertheless, if a balance is to be kept then at least some allowance must be made for displacement.

A number of studies have been completed which have examined not just the number of employment opportunities opened up by job creation, but also the way in which the participants have reacted to such experience[2]. Most studies have concluded that while relatively few participants joined job creation projects because of the positive attraction of the opportunity (most joined projects because nothing else, in particular no other regular work, was available and job creation was seen as being "better than the dole") once on a

project they reacted generally favourably to their
experience. This might be exemplified by reference to the findings from a research project that
looked at both the Job Creation and Work
Experience Programme with which the author was
associated. This research project[3] sought the
views of about 1,000 participants on the two
programmes on their experience, initially while on
their project. Generally, it was found that few
respondents were actively hostile towards the
projects (see Table 6.1). For example, when they
were asked whether there was anything they liked
about about their projects only 7 per cent of the
Work Experience and 16 per cent of the Job
Creation sample were unable to find anything
positive to say. A majority of respondents from
both programmes said that they found the job they
had been given to do interesting and over a third
in each programme praised job conditions.
Similarly when asked if there was anything they
disliked about their experiences, half of the Job
Creation and two thirds of the Work Experience
respondents said that there was nothing they could
point to. Additionally, when asked if their jobs
were interesting, slightly less than half of the
Job Creation and slightly more than half of the
Work Experience respondents said that they were
interesting all or most of the time, whereas only
a small proportion said that their work was
boring. The result was a fairly high overall
satisfaction rating. In this sense this particular survey mirrored the findings of the
Manpower Services Commission's own investi-
gations. However, it is important also to record
that the survey referred to also found some less
optimistic trends. For example, there was
considerable concern about the level of work
provided on projects: there was a strong feeling
that it demanded no particular skills and 'could
have been done by anyone'. Similarly, concern
was expressed about the level and relevance of the
training offered on projects and about the level
of remuneration offered (particularly in the case
of the respondents on the Work Experience Programme); a substantial body of respondents felt
that they were a source of 'cheap labour' for
employers (and 40 per cent of respondents on the
Work Experience Programme made this particular
comment).

Table 6.1:   Summary of Selected Responses to Work
             Creation Programmes

	JCP		WEP	
POSITIVE COMMENTS	No.	%	No.	%
Positive comment made	607	83.6	232	92.8
No positive comment made	119	16.4	18	7.2
Total	726	100.0	250	100.0
NEGATIVE COMMENTS				
Negative comment made	364	50.1	81	32.4
No negative comment made	362	49.9	169	67.6
Total	726	100.0	250	100.0
INTEREST VALUE OF PROJECT				
Interesting all or most of the time	320	48.2	138	55.2
Fairly interesting but dull patches	278	38.3	93	37.2
Boring or uninteresting	97	13.4	19	7.6
Don't know	1	0.1	0	0.0
Total	726	100.0	250	100.0
OVERALL EVALUATION OF PROJECT				
Very satisfied	95	13.1	44	17.6
Satisfied	449	61.8	168	67.2
Just acceptable	123	16.9	24	9.6
Dissatisfied	51	7.0	11	4.4
Very dissatisfied	8	1.1	3	1.2
Total	726	100.0	250	100.0

Source:
M P Jackson, V Hanby, 'Work Creation Programmes:
Participant Responses', Industrial Relations
Journal, Vol.10, No.2, 1979, p.27.

The concern that participants in job creation programmes might be used as a source of cheap labour has been echoed in comment outside the confines of this particular survey. For example, this issue was highlighted in a recent study by Youth Aid[4]. In that study it was noted that the majority of projects in the Work Experience on Employers' Premises branch of the Youth Opportunity Programme were concentrated in small, low paying, non-unionised work places. 'Rather than philanthropic employers "helping" the young unemployed and providing additional places to their normal workforce, it was increasingly argued that they were using YOP to subsidise their recruitment and screening procedures, if not directly exploiting young employees as cheap labour'[5]. One of the reasons why abuses may have crept into the operation of job creation schemes is that insufficient resources have been provided to enable effective monitoring.

It is not easy to accurately measure the effectiveness of job creation programmes in counteracting the undesirable consequences of unemployment, but some guidelines can be provided. It seems reasonable to argue that job creation projects can halt the undesirable consequences of unemployment while people are on a project. Engagement on a project, for example, demands that participants adhere to regular working hours and this may be expected to halt the drift to a psychological state that makes a person in practice unemployable. Similarly, engagement on a project at least means that the boredom associated with not having a regular work task to complete will be relieved: it may also be expected to persuade participants that there is hope that their positions will improve in the future (in many cases job creation programme participation has been advertised as a stepping stone to normal employment). There is a reasonable amount of research evidence to support at least some of these assumptions. For example, surveys of young people on the Youth Opportunities Programme[6] have shown that participation protected young people from the psychologically detrimental effects of unemployment, in the short term. However, the same surveys have suggested that these beneficial effects were only short term unless participation on the Programme was followed swiftly by normal employment. Thus, it was found that young people who were unemployed after the Youth Opportunities Programme reported the same psychological symptoms as other unemployed young people who had not been on the Programme.

There are, also a number of other caveats to be added. For example, most young people who join a job creation project appear to be doing work which under normal circumstances they would not have chosen and in many cases they do not intend to continue in such work after job creation. The value of this experience as specific work preparation, therefore is questionable. At best it is an acceptable but relatively unimportant interlude: in some cases it may be a way of "cooling out" job aspirations. Similarly, but potentially more important, job creation may be simply an interlude in a period of prolonged unemployment. Some young people are unemployed for the whole of the period between school and job creation and then return to the ranks of the unemployed after job creation. There is an obvious danger that such young people will feel that they have been misled and believe that job creation was simply a way of temporarily removing them from the unemployment register, say for straight forward party political reasons. Such cynicism, may mean that those concerned see less hope for the future than they did before they joined a job creation project and that they have less trust in the ability of the traditional political system to meet their needs. The number of young people for which job creation has simply been such an interlude in an otherwise prolonged period of unemployment has increased rather than decreased in recent years.

The second aim of job creation programmes, as outlined above, has been to improve the chances of participants gaining normal employment in the future. In the early days of the programmes a substantial proportion of participants found permanent employment fairly soon after leaving a project. In the case of the Job Creation and Work Experience Programmes about 50 per cent of participants in the former and over 70 per cent of participants in the latter found permanent employment either immediately after leaving their project, or within a few months after. Evidence from the early years of the Youth Opportunities Programme showed similarly healthy post project employment rates. For example, a survey of people entering the Youth Opportunities Programme between September and October 1978 found that about 70 per cent of participants managed to find employment within a few weeks of leaving their project. However, even in those early years there were a few clouds on the horizon. For instance, it seemed that one of the reasons for the high post project employment rates of young people participating in the Work Experience Programme was that participants were carefully selected by sponsors and in many cases sponsors used the programme as a way of further screening potential recruits before taking them on to their normal workforce. Similarly, post project employment rates varied widely from one type of project to another and from one Programme to another. For example, in the case of the Job Creation and Work Experience Programmes projects connected with the distributive trades, education, social work and research provided the best subsequent employment figures; in the case of the Youth Opportunities Programme, Work Experience on Employers' Premises Projects seemed to do best[7]. If Programmes rather than projects are compared then, for example, the Youth Opportunities Programme did better than the Special Temporary Employment Programme (while the post project employment rates for the Youth Opportunities Programme were about 60 per cent for those entering the programme in 1979, they were about 45 per cent in the case of the Special Temporary Employment Programme and they have been less than 20 per cent in the case of the Community Enterprise Programme).

It is more important to record, though, that in recent years the post project employment rates of even the most successful job creation programmes have dropped significantly. For example, surveys by the Manpower Services Commission in January and March 1981 found that only 37 and 36 per cent of participants on the Youth Opportunities Programmes respectively gained employment immediately after leaving a project, and only another 3 and 2 per cent (of the January and March surveys respectively) found employment within the following five months. It is difficult not to conclude that as youth unemployment has risen the effectiveness of job creation programmes in this matter has been severely reduced. Job creation projects, at their best, may help participants to compete more effectively in the labour market, but this may be less valuable than anticipated if there are no jobs to compete for.

It is also important to recognise that figures relating to the post project employment rates of participants of job creation programmes are not necessarily a measure of the effectiveness of such programmes in this matter. Although most participants experienced a spell of unemployment before joining a job creation programme, in some cases the spell was a short one and in other cases participants also had experience of normal work. It would not be unreasonable to assume, then, that at least some of the job creation participants would have obtained employment even if they had not joined a programme. It would be impossible to assess accurately how much post project employment could be directly attributed to job creation experience and how much to other factors. Nevertheless, it is worthwhile pointing out that some surveys have shown that job creation participants who gain employment after leaving a project generally are those who anyway might have been expected to have been most successful in the labour market (that is, for instance, those with the best qualifications and those with fathers from a relatively high social class)[8].

Earlier it was noted that in many cases young people who joined job creation projects had no intention of seeking permanent work in the same area. Of course, some of them have had to revise their ideas after leaving job creation projects and many of them have done so when they have been offered permanent work by the project sponsor. However, many others have not done so. The value of job creation experience as far as future employment has been concerned then has been limited to the ability to show a prospective employer acceptance of work disciplines rather than specific relevant work skills. Further, there is a great deal of evidence that while the standard of training on job creation projects has improved over the years, it still leaves a lot to be desired. In many cases training seems to have been limited. In the Community Enterprise Programme, for example, a special budget was established of £1.6 million a year from which sponsors could reclaim the costs of approved off-the-job training and education. In fact only a small proportion of this training budget was used and the element of education and training on schemes generally was small (of course, there were exceptions, but they were not the rule). Explanations for the failure to use the full budget available have included the administrative difficulties involved in claiming the additional financial support and the absence of encouragement from the MSC to do so.

The third aim of many job creation programmes has been to produce something of value to the community. Earlier it was noted that this aim has not been shared by all programmes: in Britain it has been a particular feature of those programmes dealing with the older age ranges (usually over 18 years of age). In practice, it is extremely difficult to measure the quality of the output of job creation programmes. The impression has been gained though that the quality of the output has improved over time. In the early years it seems that the desire to 'get projects off the ground' quickly meant that some projects which might not have been accepted were financed: examples were widely reported of, for instance, projects that did little more than involve participants in counting the number of manhole covers. To some extent the problems faced in the early years have receded although in some parts of the country the shortage of sponsors has been a problem that has occurred throughout the history of different programmes.

It is not surprising that official descriptions of projects have concentrated on what have been considered to be the successes. For example, a description of a project to help the elderly in Derbyshire has been given which shows a clear community benefit.

> Derbyshire County are employing 25 young people on a project to provide practical and inexpensive help to the elderly who are at risk during the winter. A simple training programme is being carried out so that young people can be employed on various tasks in the homes of elderly people. These include eliminating draught through insulation, checking for damp, checking heating appliances to ensure that they are safe and give sufficient heat, providing safe low-voltage electric blankets to the bedridden and making a room as near 21°C as possible[9].

On the other hand job creation programmes have been the subject of considerable criticism: some of this has suggested that the work completed simply has been of benefit to the sponsor and has produced nothing of benefit to the community at large. For example, a number of trade unions have expressed concern of this kind about a number of Youth Opportunities Programme projects. They have also claimed that on occasions there has been flagrant abuse by sponsors: for instance, where participants have been used to decorate employers' homes.

It might also be noted that at times the objective that job creation projects should produce something of value for the community at large has been in conflict with other objectives. For example, emphasis on community benefit has led to a concentration on projects in the environmental and construction areas, yet such an emphasis may mean that work experience and training is being offered in a sector that is already in decline and where the acquisition of skilled jobs normally demands extensive vocational training beyond the scope of job creation projects. Similarly, concentration on such projects may lead to an unwelcome bias in recruitment: few opportunities exist on these projects for females.

The frequent changes in the provisions of job creation programmes means that a general evaluation of the kind attempted above will be only a rough guide that may point out some broad lessons. Further little has been said so far specifically about the most recent job creation programme, the Community Programme. This is because at the time of writing the programme was relatively new and there was no research evidence on its operation. However, a number of the comments made about the Programme after its announcement might be touched on briefly.

The Unemployment Unit has suggested three major objections to the Programme[10]. The first is that a better programme could have been provided at lower cost. Specifically, it has been argued that the Community Enterprise Programme could have been expanded to provide the same number of additional jobs at no greater net expenditure cost. Such a strategy would have been preferable because participants on the Community Enterprise Programme were paid a higher wage than the proposals for the Community

Programme: these higher wages, it has been argued, would not have resulted in a higher net cost because they would have reduced the need to claim benefits like Family Income Supplement. The second objection is that the programme will encourage low wages. Thus, it was stated that the 'Government's refusal to expand CEP is based only on their determination to cut wage levels'[11]. The wage levels to be paid on the Community Programme it was argued, were to be subject to a maximum which is lower than many similar jobs would offer and would exclude the possibility of increasing earnings by overtime or bonuses. The third objection to the Programme was that there is no real provision for training: sponsors who spend extra money on training will have to do so by reducing wage costs.

Of course, by no means everyone accepts the view of the Programme put forward by the Unemployment Unit. Specifically some of the Unit's arguments have been challenged by the Manpower Services Commission[12]. They argue, for example, that the net cost of expanding the Community Enterprise Programme, would have been higher than assumed by the Unemployment Unit and higher than the net cost of the Community Programme. They also argue that the Programme will not encourage low wages, in part because only work which would not otherwise have been undertaken will be provided and because trade unions will be able to check locally that the safeguards have been applied. However, there must be some doubts about this argument. The safeguards are less impressive that at first sight: 'the rule is that work can be done which would not otherwise be done for two years. Cuts in local authority services have now been going on for so long that essential services of two years can now be done under CP.'[13] It also needs to be borne in mind that Government ministers have made no secret of their view that high wage levels are a cause of unemployment: it would not be inconsistent of them, then, to hope that a venture like the Community Programme could help to reduce wage levels.

Youth Training

There has long been recognition of the need to review the provision of training for young people

in Britain. Comparisons frequently have been
made with the position in countries like West
Germany where an integrated system of vocational
education and training has been available for many
years. In their 1981 Consultative Document on
training the Manpower Services Commission pointed
out that whereas in the UK 44 per cent of those
who completed compulsory schooling received no
further education or training, in France the
figure was only 19 per cent and in West Germany
only 7 per cent. The need to take action has
been heightened by the decline in the traditional
apprenticeship system. In the last decade the
annual average apprenticeship intake has been
halved to about 60,000.

In this sense, then, the proposals for the
Youth Training Scheme, were made to a receptive
audience. There was widespread belief that an
initiative was long-overdue. However, the
proposals in practice brought a mixed response,
and outright hostility from some quarters.
Undoubtedly one of the reasons for the hostility
was that the way the original proposals were put
forward by Norman Tebbit in the White Paper
encouraged suspicion of motives. In particular,
the proposals for the level of allowance and the
threat of compulsion implied by the withholding of
supplementary benefit encouraged the belief that
the real objective of the initiative was not to
provide a better system of youth training but to
foster other aspects of the Government economic
policy. In hindsight it seems that such fears
may not have been totally misplaced. A 'leaked'
report from the Central Policy Review Staff
suggested that the 'genesis of the scheme lay as
much as anything else in a concern to take 16
year-olds off a jobless register which would have
otherwise reached unacceptably high levels; to
contain the street crime bred by lengthening dole
queues; and to force down youth wages in keeping
with the Government's overall economic
strategy'[14]. Of course, the detailed proposals
for the Youth Training Scheme represented a
considerable modification of the original CPRS
ideas and were developed by a tripartite working
group which included trade union representatives
as members. Nevertheless, fears about the
original objectives of the scheme undoubtedly have
coloured reactions to it. It is clear, though,
that the objections voiced go beyond simply this

general scepticism about objectives. A number of
detailed objections can be listed.

First, it has been suggested that the scheme
as a whole, and in particular the training to be
offered, are biased towards the needs of employers
rather than young people. The statements of
David Young, the Chairman of the MSC, have
encouraged such views. Outlining the advantages
of the scheme to employers he said:

> You now have the opportunity to take on
> young men or women, train them and let them
> work for you almost entirely at our expense
> and then decide whether to employ them[15].

The bias towards employers' needs may be
linked to the problem of attracting sufficient
places. In the early stages of setting up the
scheme there were fears that it might be difficult
to attract sufficient places. In fact by the end
of 1983 the MSC claimed that they were close to
meeting their targets: 440,511 places had been
approved, and another 5,710 were 'firmly anticipated' compared to a planned total of 459,770.

Second, there has been concern about the
likely quality of the training offered. The
scheme demands 13 weeks 'off-the-job' training and
in many cases the training will be provided by
further education and training colleges. However,
provision of adequate training is expensive, and
at the time of writing the MSC was only allowing
£550 to cover induction, training and supervision
costs (in the spring of 1984 it was announced that
the block grant paid to managing agents of mode A
schemes would be increased by 5 per cent to £2,050
from 1st September 1984 though the allocation of
the block grant between the different elements
still had to be decided). Employers may 'top up'
the MSC money to enable adequate training to be
provided but there is no requirement for them to
do so. Further there is no obligation on
employers to use the facilities for training
available in the public sector. Employers can
use their own training facilities or they can
contract the work out to private enterprise. The
controls that will be placed on such training will
be few: in particular there will be no requirement that instructors need to have been trained
themselves or qualified.

Third, there has been concern about the extent
to which schemes will be monitored to prevent
abuse by sponsors. Clearly the role of trade
unions will be important. The TUC has been
directly involved in setting up the scheme at a
national level and at the local and area level
union representatives will have the opportunity to
monitor (and in certain circumstances to veto)
provision. Nevertheless, concern remains about
whether trade unions will be able to be effective
enough in this role. This concern arises, in
part, because of the difficulties unions have
faced in attempting to monitor and control abuse
in other special employment programmes.

Related to this there is concern about the
extent to which the Youth Training Scheme will be
used as a substitute for the normal employment of
young people. This concern has been heightened
because of the way that the Scheme has been
established. The Task Group set up by the MSC to
discuss the proposals put forward by the Government sought to increase the coverage of the Scheme
but, in an attempt to keep the Scheme within the
cost bounds established, it introduced the
'additionality' principle. Most schemes are run
by managing agents (71 per cent of young people in
schemes in April 1984 were in ones run by managing
agents - usually referred to as 'Mode A' schemes)
and the majority of these are ordinary employers. Managing agents are expected to take on
three extra employees for every two normal
recruits and normally all five are YTS trainees.
It was felt that this would make the scheme
attractive to employers, because they would be
paid for a number of young people they would have
taken on anyway. However, it also meant that
they could be offered a lower sum per trainee and
this meant the total cost could be kept within
acceptable bounds. As far as substitution is
concerned it created a major problem because the
additionality principle builds substitution into
the scheme. Raffe has argued that the structure
of Mode A Schemes is such that substitution
'cannot be avoided merely by an emphasis on tight
monitoring'. He goes on to say that the additionality principle is 'potentially ambiguous',
'hard to police' and it will become increasingly
so over time as the definition of firms normal
intakes becomes more and more arbitrary'[16].
Many trade unions are particularly worried about

the substitution effect of YTS. They see
employers being encouraged to use YTS because of
the cost savings, and the effect being the
replacement of the wage that the young person
might have expected to receive by the YTS
allowance.

Fourth, there is concern about the effect of
the Youth Training Scheme on the traditional
education system. Its introduction may mean that
young people who might have considered staying on
at school to go into the sixth form will not do so
and as a result sixth forms may become more
elitist. Such fears are clearly expressed in the
following quotation.

Many people working in the schools sector
fear that one effect of the introduction of
YTS will be that school sixth forms will
become the preserve of the academic
elite. Those who wish to acquire high
status qualifications - basically GCE O and
A levels - will remain at school. Others
attracted by the training allowance and the
hope that the period of work experience
will give them 'a foot in the door' in the
fight for employment will go for a
traineeship....

As far as the schools are concerned the
sixth form will become more of a middle
class enclave striving towards the academic
values imposed by the higher education
system. If that happens we might well see
it followed by a knock-on effect on the
lower school curriculum, further reinforcing academic values and further activating
those who do not share those values and
will all the more readily embrace the
opportunity for getting out of the
education system at the earliest opportunity. And if participation rates
amongst the 16-19 age group do drop then
such is our topsy-turvey system of resourcing that there will then be repercussions
on the whole staffing and resourcing available for the secondary school system[17].

At the same time the fear exists that the
effort being put into developing vocational training outside schools may draw attention away from

141

moves that have started to change the normal
school curriculum and make it more relevant to the
needs of those leaving school at the minimum age.

As well as these detailed concerns there is a
more general one which mirrors an anxiety felt
over the job creation programmes. This concern
is that at the end of the period on a special
employment programme many participants will be
unable to find work. In this case, training
itself does not produce jobs. It may make it
easier for young people to compete in the labour
market but if there are no jobs available to
compete for it will simply be producing what has
been referred to as 'a better class of unemployed
teenager'. Such a situation could lead to young
people adopting a cynical attitude towards the
Youth Training Scheme and as such it could exacer-
bate the social and political problems it is meant
to alleviate. Such a situation could also mean
that the value of youth training as a whole will
be underestimated and reaction against the
specific experience of the Youth Training Scheme
could set back the more general cause of youth
training.

However, it also needs to be recorded that
despite such criticism of the Youth Training
Scheme there have been those (not simply Government representatives) who have been willing to
defend it, and those who have opposed aspects of
it have disagreed over the strategy that should be
adopted towards it[18]. A section of the labour
movement has argued for outright opposition to the
scheme. Others, though have been more cautious
and have suggested simply that an attempt should
be made to change aspects of the scheme and to
closely monitor its operation. In practice
despite considerable heart searching this latter
view has dominated.

Subsidies

Two subsidies specifically directed at young
people were introduced in the mid 1970s. The
first of these, the Recruitment Subsidy for School
Leavers, was introduced in 1975. A survey commissioned by the Department of Employment in March
1976 sought to determine the effectiveness of the
scheme[19]. The survey was carried out by Marplan
and covered all firms claiming the subsidy for
five or more people as well as one in ten of all

firms claiming the subsidy for less than five people. Two important conclusions were reached. The first was that a large proportion of firms would have recruited just as many young people had the subsidy not been on offer. Thus, 76 per cent of firms said that they would have recruited as many school leavers without the subsidy, and it was thought that even some of the 24 per cent of firms that said their recruitment plan would have been different without the subsidy would still have taken on some school leavers: taking this into account it was thought that the additional recruitment of school leavers because of the subsidy was within the 15 to 20 per cent range, or around 5,000 young people. The second conclusion was that in some cases firms reduced their recruitment of other groups to enable them to recruit young people. 14 per cent of firms stated that they had adopted this strategy: in most cases, though the young people were substituting for part-time workers.

The conclusion reached as a result of the survey was that 'a general subsidy of this type for school leavers has very little effect in terms of the 'additional' recruitment it brings about'[20]. Nevertheless, in a review of this research it was suggested that as 'unemployment amongst young people in general continues to be a problem it can be maintained that special help should be concentrated on the least advantaged amongst this age group'[21]. It was this kind of conclusion, that the subsidy should be more targeted, that led the government to replace the Recruitment Subsidy for School Leavers with the Youth Employment Subsidy in October 1976. As has already been indicated this subsidy was much more tightly targeted being designed to encourage employers to recruit young people aged under 20 who had been continuously unemployed for at least 6 months.

The Department of Employment carried out a preliminary survey of the operation of the new subsidy in July and August 1977, and a follow up survey in September of the same year. The survey concentrated on employers[22], and as with the research into the impact of the earlier subsidy sought to determine how many new jobs were created as a result of the financial assistance given. The conclusion was that about one in eight of all jobs for which the subsidy was given would not

have been available at all had it not been for the
subsidy. The survey also sought to examine the
extent to which the subsidy encouraged the employment of disadvantaged groups as opposed to other
groups, even though the job itself was not a net
addition. In this case it was found that a
further one in eight jobs would not have been
given to a member of the target groups had it not
been for the subsidy. The conclusion drawn from
the survey was that 'in its main aim, to encourage
employers to give preference to long-term unemployed young people, the scheme had some effect,
and in addition led to the creation of some
employment that did not exist before'.[23]
However, it must be recorded that the percentages
referred to from the survey suggest that this
effect was fairly small and that this subsidy was
very little improvement on the previous scheme.

Employment subsidies for the young were
revived in 1982 when the government introduced the
Young Workers Scheme. The details of the scheme
differed from those of earlier subsidies in a
number of ways, though most importantly in that
help was restricted to low wage jobs. Evidence
of the impact of the scheme suggests a similar
pattern to earlier subsidy packages as far as the
creation of extra jobs is concerned. The Department of Employment has estimated that 77 per cent
of the jobs would have been filled even if the
subsidy had not existed. Further in about 12 per
cent of cases young people engaged under the
scheme were with the same employer as when participating in the Youth Opportunities Programme[24].

While the net additional employment created by
the subsidy seems to have been small, it is less
clear what effect the subsidy has had in another
area, the level of wages paid to young people.
It has been widely suggested that the scheme was
devised by the Prime Minister's Special adviser
Professor Alan Walters to try to help to reduce
the level of youth wages. The restriction of the
subsidy to low wage employment may have had this
effect not simply in the subsidised jobs but more
widely: taken together with the Youth Training
Scheme, the Young Workers Scheme seems likely to
have had a major impact on the earned income of
young people.

The Impact of Special Employment Measures

Early Retirement

Early retirement can, and has, been justified on a variety of different grounds, many of which will have nothing to do directly with youth unemployment. In the case of many early retirement measures in both the public and private sector the aim simply has been to shed staff and the only effect that this is likely to have had on youth unemployment, is that to the extent it means that other workers will not be made redundant, it will not make things worse. However, it is clear that one of the reasons for official encouragement of early retirement, and for the introduction, in particular, of the job release scheme, was the hope that it would enable other people, including young people, to fill the vacancies.

The Department of Employment has commissioned research to assess the extent to which the Job Release Scheme leads to people from the unemployment register finding employment through the "replacement effect". The research was based on a sample of 500 former employers of people who had taken advantage of the Job Release Scheme and was completed in the latter part of 1980[25]. In summary it was found that in 60 per cent of cases it could be stated that a replacement had been hired and that this had led to a person on the unemployment register being offered a job by the company. In 32 per cent of the total number of cases the person taken on from the unemployment register was a direct replacement for the person joining the Job Release Scheme: the balance of 28 per cent were indirect replacements. However, in 40 per cent of the cases it was stated that it was not possible to say that an unemployed person had obtained a job with the company as a result of the exercise. In a number of cases the post of the person joining the Job Release Scheme was not filled at all, in other cases it was filled by someone not unemployed at the time, and in still other cases the outcome was still not determined. The researchers argued that in a number of these instances it was reasonable to assume that even though an unemployed person was not given a job in the company from which the applicant to the Job Release Scheme retired, an unemployed person may still have benefited and found employment as a result of the exercise, with another employer. For example, if the original company engaged an employed person to fill the vacancy of the person retiring then it may be that an unemployed person would be hired by the second company to fill the post of the person who left. If all such factors and possibilities were taken into account, it was argued, in practice the Job Release Scheme might have led to a reduction in unemployment in about 85 per cent of all cases.

This research clearly does not allow one to measure exactly the precise effect of the Job Release Scheme on youth unemployment. However, it would be reasonable to assume that at least some of the replacements were young people though the extent to which this has been true in particular instances will have varied with the precise nature of the job vacated. In some cases the job will not have been one that a young person reasonably could have expected to fill: in such instances it seems probable that young people are most likely to have been affected by the vacancy where there has been an indirect rather than a direct replacement.

Conclusions

The special employment measures used in Britain to try to deal with youth unemployment have had mixed fortunes. The job creation programmes have provided temporary employment opportunities for substantial numbers of young people, but the proportion of participants who have found jobs afterwards has declined steeply in recent years raising questions about the effectiveness of such measures in a period of rapidly rising unemployment. The need to expand and improve the quality of training given to young people has been widely recognised: however, the most recent and the most substantial initiative in this area, the Youth Training Scheme has had to face considerable criticism. Subsidies and measures to reduce the size of the active labour force, similarly, have been far from an unquestioned success.

There are, then, a range of questions and doubts about the detailed operation and effectiveness of the special employment measures. In some instances it is clear that the measures have not met the hopes of their sponsors. For example, it was claimed that the proportion of participants on the Youth Opportunities Programme who would gain

employment after leaving the programme would be
far higher than turned out to be the case. As well, though, questions need to be asked of
a more general nature about the direction of the
overall strategy. For example, to what extent is
a strategy which aims simply to take people out of
the labour market for a temporary period justified
in the current economic climate? Again questions
need to be asked about the implications of giving
responsibility for an initiative with major implications for education and training to a labour
market agency. It is to questions of this kind
that the next chapter turns.

Notes

1. See for example, M Faulkner, Direct Job
   Creation in the Member States of the European
   Community, EEC Brussels, 1978, Study
   No.77/15; D Karsten, Job Creation Schemes in
   the European Community, E.E.C. Brussels, Study
   No.80/40; G E Johnson, J Q Tunda, An Impact
   Evaluation of the Public Employment Programme,
   U.S. Department of Labor, Office of Assistant
   Secretary for Policy Evaluation and Research,
   Washington, 1974.
2. See for example, M P Jackson, V J B Hanby,
   British Work Creation Programmes, Gower,
   Aldershot, 1982; M H Banks, C Mullings,
   E J Jackson 'A Bench Mark for Youth Opportun-
   ities', Employment Gazette, March 1983,
   pp.91-5; and surveys by the Manpower Services
   Commission reported regularly by the Special
   Programmes Division.
3. M P Jackson, V J B Hanby, ibid.
4. Youthaid, Quality or Collapse? Youthaid
   Review of the Youth Opportunities Programme,
   Youthaid, London 1981.
5. D Finn, 'Youth Unemployment and Politics',
   Youth and Policy, Spring 1983, p.19.
6. See E M Stafford, P R Jackson, M H Banks,
   'Employment, Work Involvement and Mental
   Illness in Less Qualified Young People',
   Journal of Occupational Psychology, 1980,
   Vol 53, pp.291-304; E M Stafford 'The Impact
   of the Youth Opportunities Programme on Young
   People's Employment Prospects and
   Psychological Well Being', British Journal of
   Guidance and Counselling, 1982, Vol 10,
   pp.12-21; M H Banks, P R Jackson,

'Unemployment and the Risk of Minor Psychological Disorder in Young People', _Psychological Medicine_, 1982, Vol 12, pp.789-98.

7. D O'Connor, 'Probabilities of Employment After Work Experience', _Employment Gazette_, January 1982, pp.8-11; L Davies, T Bedeman, S Harvey, 'What Happens After YOP - A Longer Term View', _Employment Gazette_, January 1982, pp.12-14; M P Jackson, V J B Hanby, op cit.

8. For evidence on the employment experiences of disadvantaged groups after job creation projects see M P Jackson, V J B Hanby op cit; T Bedeman, J Harvey, _Young People on YOP - A National Survey of Entrants to the Youth Opportunities Programme_, MSC, London, 1982, Research and Development Series No.3; T Bedeman, G Courtney, 'Taking the Opportunity', _Employment Gazette_, October, 1982; P Jones, 'Effects of Rising Unemployment on School Leavers', _Employment Gazette_, January, 1983, pp.13-16; M H Banks, C Mullings, E J Jackson op cit tried to assess the overall impact of the Youth Opportunities Programme on future employment chances. They concluded that the programme had a positive but limited effect in the long term.

9. _Department of Employment Gazette_, March, 1977, p.212.

10. See Unemployment Unit Briefing, No.4, August, 192.

11. _Ibid_ p.5.

12. Reply to Unemployment Unit by the Manpower Services Commission. Published by the Unemployment Unit in a revised edition of Briefing No.4.

13. _Ibid_ p.vi3.

14. _Sunday Times_, 22 May, 1983, p.69.

15. Socialism and Education, Editorial, _Journal of the Socialist Education Association_, Vol.10, No.1.

16. _Ibid_ p.6. D Raffe, 'Youth Unemployment and the MSC: 1977-1983' in D McClone, _The Scottish Government Yearbook 1984_, Unit for the Study of Government in Scotland, Edinburgh, 1983, p.215.

17. In the issue of Socialism and Education referred to above (Vol.10, No.1), for example, while the general argument was hostile to the Youth Training Scheme, John Randall, Assistant

General Secretary of the Civil Service Union, broadly welcomed the initiative and in particular argued that education and training ought to be kept apart.

18. See Department of Employment Gazette, July, 1977, p.696.
19. Ibid p.696.
20. Ibid p.696.
21. Department of Employment Gazette, April, 1978, pp.424-5.
22. Ibid p.425.
23. Hansard, 22 December, 1982, written answers columns 595-7.
24. Department of Employment Gazette, May, 1982, pp.196-9.

Chapter Seven

YOUTH UNEMPLOYMENT: THE STRATEGY AND ITS
IMPLICATIONS

The Strategy for Dealing with Youth Unemployment

The rise in the level of youth unemployment and
its emergence as a major cause for concern has
been one of the most important political and
social developments of recent years. Governments
of all political persuasions have been keen to
show that they have shared the general concern,
that they have had compassion for the plight of
the unemployed, and that they have been doing what
they could to deal with the problem. As has been
argued earlier, this does not mean that youth
unemployment, or for that matter unemployment in
general, always has had the highest priority on
the political agenda, nor that at times
governments have not pursued policies which have
exacerbated rather than eased the problem.
Nevertheless, it is still the case that governments have been keen to show concern and to be
able to claim that they have been taking some
action to deal with the problem.
    In practice the action taken has relied very
heavily on what are referred to as 'special
employment measures'. This has been true both in
the case of unemployment as a whole and youth
unemployment in particular. The variety of
special employment measures introduced to deal
with youth unemployment have been outlined and
some of the detailed considerations of their
operation have been reviewed. It might be
worthwhile at this juncture, however, looking more
generally at the basis of the overall strategy.
    The major thrust of the strategy of using
special employment measures has been in three
directions. First, it has been to create addi-

tional employment on a temporary basis. This has been most clearly the aim in the case of the job creation measures. Although on occasions such measures have been used to create long term employment opportunities, say by providing pump priming finance for new developments, generally this has not been the case. The assumption has been that the provision of temporary employment opportunities in itself is valuable. They allow a person to be taken off the unemployment register and may halt the development of the undesirable social and political consequences of long term unemployment that have been noted. In this way they may help an unemployed person retain the interest and capacity to obtain normal employment "once the economy revives" and such employment becomes more generally available.

The second thrust of the strategy of special employment measures has been to try to reduce the size of the active labour force. The introduction of early retirement schemes, like the Job Release Scheme, clearly fit into such a category. While such measures by reducing the competition for what jobs have been available may be seen to assist anyone seeking work and therefore are not meant simply to benefit one age group, clearly the young can benefit from such devices and in the past it has frequently been argued that they would do so.

The third thrust of the strategy of using special employment measures has been to encourage training and re-training. In practice this aim overlaps with the other two. In many instances job creation schemes have been linked to training, and participation in a training scheme at least temporarily removes a person from the labour market. However, training programmes, like the Youth Training Scheme, ostensibly also have the specific and dominant aim of preparing young people so that they can better meet the demands of the labour market and thereby better compete in it.

In practice, the strategy adopted raises a number of important questions. Two might be highlighted. The first is the extent to which the continuing emphasis on the provision of short term job opportunities is a useful part of the strategy. When the first job creation schemes were introduced in the early/mid 1970s governments and many economic forecasters still hoped that the decline in employment opportunities would be a short term phenomenon. In such circumstances a case could be made for providing those out of work with employment on a temporary basis in the hope that this experience would help them re-enter the normal labour market when the up-turn in the economy occurred. In fact, few would now argue that high unemployment is likely to be a short term phenomenon: most forecasts recognise that overall unemployment and youth unemployment, are likely to remain at a high level for at least the medium term future.

This re-assessment of the future economic climate means that the role of job creation schemes and similar attempts to produce short term job opportunities is less clear. Job creation schemes and the like essentially represent a "holding operation". While some young people might benefit from such a strategy it seems that in general a "holding operation" is no longer appropriate. If the assumption is made that in the medium term the level of youth unemployment will remain unacceptably high, then if special employment measures, like job creation and related schemes, are to make more than merely a marginal contribution to the problem, the basis of their operation will need to be changed. Much more emphasis will need to be placed on using special employment measures to create long term employment opportunities, say by seeing them as "pump priming" devices.

Already a number of other countries have moved in such a direction. For example, in a number of West European countries, like France and Belgium, moves have been made to use special employment measures to create longer term opportunities in the "third sector" of employment. This is usually taken to mean employment, often along co-operative lines, on tasks that may be of community benefit but currently are not undertaken either by the private or the public sector. In other countries, like Canada, the use of special employment measures as pump priming for employment opportunities designed to last after the withdrawal of outside financial support, has been common for some time. The extent to which such measures can be expected to cope with a problem of youth unemployment on the scale currently being faced is debateable, but at least it can be argued that if high levels of youth unemployment are a

long term problem they represent a more rational
use of special employment measures.

It is important to stress, however, that the
issue here is not simply one of ensuring that the
policy has positive benefits. It is arguable
that if the direction is not changed then the
policy will not simply be ineffective but it may,
in fact, have negative implications. A policy
which seems to offer young people little more than
an interlude in a period of otherwise prolonged
unemployment may be regarded by the young themselves as little more than a cynical political
manoeuvre. If their hopes are raised only to be
dashed again they may become more rather than less
bitter and more rather than less resentful of the
current political system. Similarly, there are
dangers that others who do not participate
directly in such schemes but have links with them
may view such schemes in a parallel fashion. For
example, groups who play an important role in
supporting and encouraging special employment
measures may become sceptical of their real value
and may withdraw support.

The second important question that is raised
by the strategy adopted is the assumptions it
contains about the causes of youth unemployment.
In the mid 1970s the balance of special employment
measures was towards subsidies and job creation:
since then the balance has changed and moved
towards training and work experience. This has
been particularly so in the case of young
people. It was quite possible to read into the
balance of measures adopted in the mid 1970s an
assumption that the high levels of youth unemployment were a temporary problem outside the control
of the young themselves. The prescriptions of
subsidies and short term job creation assumed that
in 'normal' economic circumstances many, or even
most, of the young people then unemployed would be
able to find a job. Such an assumption cannot be
read into the current balance of special employment measures. On the contrary, the assumption
must be that the high level of youth unemployment
has a great deal to do with the young people themselves: they are being trained or re-trained
because they do not meet the needs of industry.

In practice, the thinking that underlies such
assumptions contains a number of different elements. For example, it seems to blame both the
victim and the traditional educational system.

153

The victim, the young person, is to blame for not having developed the kind of skills and personal characteristics that employers find acceptable; the educational system is similarly to blame for not encouraging, or even requiring, the young person to develop these skills and characteristics and concentrating instead on more academic but less relevant areas. The solutions put forward, which follow from this kind of analysis, are to offer the young person a relevant training package and to seek to change the basis of at least part of the educational system. The introduction of measures like the Youth Training Scheme can be seen as an example directed to the first aim and the moves to introduce more work experience into the school curriculum and to enable the MSC to have a much greater say in what in the past has been seen as the province of the traditional educational system can be seen as an example of a move directed at the second aim.

The assumption outlined above, in fact, is beset with problems. There is little evidence, as has already been argued, to support the view that high levels of youth unemployment have been caused by inadequacies in the young themselves or the educational system. Rather the dominant view of researchers seems to be that the high level of youth unemployment is firmly linked to the problems facing the economic system more generally. Further, it is not clear, even if one went part of the way with the assumption that is being made, exactly what employers want from young people. Employers' needs are frequently referred to but rarely adequately defined. A report of the Central Policy Review Staff emphasised this point.

> There are quite serious difficulties about interpreting what the needs of industry are....These (needs) are far from uniform; there are inconsistencies between what employers say they want and the values implicit in their selection process; their conception of their needs is not explicit and clearly formulated[1].

In practice, what is frequently meant by employers' needs is not particular technical skills but a flexibility to adapt to change and a more acceptable "attitude" and work characteristics.

The Strategy and its Implications

It is not difficult to see, though, why despite these problems, such assumptions about the causes of youth unemployment should appear attractive to many. Finn argues, for instance, that for

Politicians of all political parties these have proved comforting arguments. If only schools turned out pupils with the right skills, the right attitudes, and a realistic sense of their labour market position, then youth unemployment would not be a problem[2].

A similar line of argument has been pursued by Markall and Gregory.

...although the notion of mismatch (between employers needs and what the young offer) critically obscures the causes of unemployment and distorts the reality of the transition from school to work it does promote certain political and ideological transformations. First, smothered in a rhetoric of social concern, it enables young people to be taken off the streets (and off the register) into colleges and onto courses thereby illustrating that the state is doing something and tackling the problem. Second, and implicitly, it locates that problem amongst the unemployed themselves. The prime focus on job finding and keeping reinforces the myth that jobs are available for those who have the skills, inclination and persistence to find and secure them. Unemployment thus becomes a matter of individual inadequacy rather than an endemic and structural feature of a contracting labour market. Third, it creates the political and ideological space which the great debate colonised and which invites new forms of statutory intervention in education and training and a re-definition of aims, objectives and methods[3].

Such criticisms do not mean that special employment measures have no role to play in a modern economy. To the contrary special employment measures can have an important role to play. However, the role may be just as impor-

tant, and arguably more important, in an expanding
as in a declining economy. In practice also, if
they are to make a real contribution to a declining economy then as much emphasis needs to be
placed on using them to aid long term job creation
as anything else. Training, by itself, or work
experience, will not create jobs and training or
work experience to be effective has to lead to
long term employment. If such long term employment for those who have been through a training or
work experience course is not simply to be at the
expense of workers who would otherwise have been
employed then efforts directed at long term job
creation, whether through more traditional demand
management techniques or special employment
measures are crucial.

The Rise of the Manpower Commission

One of the most important by-products of the
development of special employment measures has
been the increase in the size and of the importance of the Manpower Services Commission.
Established at the beginning of 1974 the
Commission was introduced by a Conservative
administration with a relatively modest budget of
some £125 million. In the mid/late 1970s and
early 1980s the budget, staff and influence of the
Commission increased enormously. Although it has
responsibility for much more than simply special
employment measures, it was developments in this
area and the response to the rising level of
unemployment, that lay behind the rapid development of the Commission into one of the most important and influential government agencies.

One of the interesting aspects of the operation of the Manpower Services Commission is the
role of the trade unions within it. Trade unions
and employers are both represented on the Commission and as a result initiatives pursued have to
receive the approval of the trade union movement
as well as the employers and the government.
This is interesting because it is one of the few
areas of government where the trade unions have
been able to play a major role since the election
of Conservative government in 1979. Generally
recent Conservative governments have isolated the
trade union movement, sought to restrict their
influence, and have made serious efforts to move
against the role of quangos. The movements

towards corporatism that were evident in the lifetime of the last Labour government seem to have
been reversed. The involvement of the trade
union movement in the Manpower Services Commssion
clearly stands out against this trend.
   In practice the trade unions have often felt
uneasy about their role on the Commission. In
recent years the trade union movement has threatened to withhold its support for a number of
proposals made from within the Commission though,
in such circumstances, it has felt itself be be in
a very difficult position. Acceptance of
proposals has limited its ability to criticise
subsequently; on the other hand, rejection of
proposals, which might give some help to the
unemployed, even those which contain unacceptable
elements, has been difficult. The kind of problems faced are illustrated in the debate over the
introduction of the Community Programme. The
following quotation shows how the TUC believed
that they had no option but to back the programme
despite, what they perceived to be, major faults.

To the delight of many of its friends, just
hours before the Chancellor of the
Exchequer rose in the House of Commons on
27 July to announce the launch of the new
"Community Programme" which will provide
130,000 temporary jobs paying an average of
£60 per week for the long term unemployed,
the TUC unexpectedly withheld endorsement
of the new scheme. The TUC view is
important because the scheme is to be run
by the MSC and therefore could not have
gone ahead without TUC endorsement.

On 14 September a TUC spokesman let it be
known that, after a prolonged debate, they
had reluctantly decided after all to
endorse the scheme. He said that the TUC
did not think it a good scheme but they
believed unemployed workers would criticise
them if they blocked any scheme which might
be of some assistance. Many of those who
have scrutinised the new scheme believe
that the TUC missed a major opportunity to
fight for the interests of the unemployed
and that they should have challenged the
Government to expand CEP (Community
Enterprise Programme)...[4].

However, the MSC has also shown that it is
willing to move against trade union opposition,
and in the case of local opposition, if necessary
to ignore it. Again, the example that is to be
quoted comes from the introduction of the Community Programme. It was recognised within the
MSC that the general acceptance of the Programme
by the TUC did not mean an end to all opposition
within the trade union movement. A number of
unions, and many branches of unions, refused to
accept the Programme in principle or decided to
impose conditions for its implementation that
would not be met. An internal MSC discussion
document on how to deal with such opposition makes
it clear that at the end of the day if persuasion
fails, then the opposition should be ignored.

We cannot allow Trade Unions to have a veto
on projects. We have then discussed the
question with the TUC who have agreed the
outline of our suggested approach to the
problem. The first requirement in any
individual case of Union opposition is to
establish whether that opposition is in
accordance with or in contravention of the
TUC guidelines. If it is within the TUC
guidelines then the task is to consider the
particular aspects of the project which are
causing difficulties and if possible to
modify them to meet the Unions' objections. In this connection it will be of
the utmost importance to ensure that only
appropriate Unions are consulted by
sponsors.

If the objections are outwith the TUC
guidance every effort should be made
locally to persuade those raising the
objections to fall in line with the TUC
position. If they refuse the case may be
referred to the Area Board for advice.
The intention in obtaining such advice
would be to establish that the scheme is in
fact within the criteria of the
Programme. If the Board finds in favour
of the project approval should be given and
the sponsor should be invited to proceed
without union approval.

Local trade union opposition to the introduction of Youth Training Scheme projects has been
met in a similar way. At the end of the day the
Manpower Services Commission has been willing to
overrule the refusal of local boards to accept
proposals.

These debates and difficulties illustrate the
problems that the trade union movement has
faced. However, they should not obscure the very
important achievement of the Commission in blunt-
ing the national opposition to the government's
strategy on youth unemployment; in practice, in
removing much of the political debate from the
area.

> In its attempts at "taking people along
> with it", we have seen that the MSC
> incorporates trade unionists and employers
> (notionally as equal partners) into its
> central, regional and local structures,
> reflecting its strategy of co-opting
> organised labour and capital in order to
> accommodate successfully particular
> economic and social strategies. And the
> political and the ideological success of
> the state's education, training and man-
> power reforms, the means whereby its
> definitions of the crisis in "the transi-
> tion from school to work" have been largely
> accepted can only be explained with refer-
> ence to the mobilisation of consent; not
> least amongst organised labour. In this
> way the question of mass youth unemploy-
> ment, for example, becomes effectively
> depoliticised. It becomes a technical/
> organisational endeavour, commitment and
> collaboration in the "national interest"
> and is most certainly not a political
> problem around production for profit and
> the free movement of capital[5].

It is important to recognise, though, that the
Manpower Services Commission has done more than
simply neutralise a great deal of the political
debate about youth unemployment. It has also, in
its moves to deal with the problems arising from
youth unemployment, made major inroads into training and education, and in so doing has introduced
a new approach to the area.

The best example to illustrate these developments is the setting up of the Youth Training Scheme, In establishing the scheme the Manpower Services Commission has been able to take over areas which traditionally have been the responsibility of the education service. Although when it set up the scheme the MSC indicated its willingness to allow the traditional education sector to participate in the provision of courses, the MSC also made it clear that it would not be content simply to act as a 'banker'. It indicated that it would monitor the kind of provision made by local authorities and in areas where local authorities failed to provide adequate courses then the MSC would establish its own. Some reports suggested that originally the MSC had planned to go even further than this and take on much more extensive powers itself, and that it might still do so in the future.

> The conviction within the DES is that Mr Young's (MSC) original proposal was that the pilot scheme (for the Youth Training Scheme) should be run from the start by the Commission itself without any attempt to involve the education service. It would have involved the establishment of 10 MSC centres - one in each region of England and Wales, the story goes - to provide full time vocational and technical education for 14 to 18 year olds.
>
> It is thought that Sir Keith (Joseph), an old friend of Mr Young, persuaded him that it was not acceptable for the Commission to set up its own state secondary school system in rivalry with the local authorities, without even giving them the chance to tackle the task.
>
> Mr Young denied that he put forward such a proposal, and insisted that he had always believed the local education authorities were the right people to run the projects if they were prepared to do so wholeheartedly. But he said that the local authority associations were right to take the implied threat in the Prime Minister's announcement seriously: if in any of the regions there was no local authority

prepared to mount a suitable project, he said, the MSC would set up an establishment of its own[6].

If the MSC were to involve itself more directly in this kind of way then there would be major implications. These would not be restricted to the kind and orientation of training given: they could extend to the structure of secondary education, for setting up of what amounted to technical schools would challenge the basis of the comprehensive system. Already the MSC has made important inroads into the traditional education sector by its sponsorship of courses: many further education and technical colleges are becoming increasingly dependent on MSC funded courses (especially given the reduction in the number of places available on the more traditional courses) with the threat that this poses to the control of the curriculum and their independence. The possibility of the introduction of technical schools, though is obviously a much more direct and more far-reaching threat.

Apart from the development of the Youth Training Scheme the MSC has also made moves which could have a similar far reaching effect on the education service with the introduction of a pilot project of technical and vocational education for 14 to 18 year olds. The pilot project is designed to provide up to 10,000 places (at a cost of about £7 million). The aim is to build a bridge between education and industry and it is meant to be a joint education/MSC initiative. However, the lead clearly has been taken by the MSC and many in the education service see it posing a threat that parallels, and reinforces, that posed by the Youth Training Scheme.

One of the important implications of the extension of the role of the MSC is the potential it offers for central control. Of course, the education service today is not free from central control, but despite the moves by central government, a significant amount of autonomy has been retained by local authorities and individual schools. There are signs that the MSC may wish to move to greater central control of the areas of education/training that it brings under its influence. An example, that might be quoted of moves in this direction comes from a letter

recently distributed by the MSC on the coverage of
"controversial" material on training courses
linked to the Youth Opportunities Programme.

I am writing to you and other trainers who
are running courses as part of the Youth
Opportunities Programme to remind you that
political and related activities are not
permitted within YOP. Particular care
should be taken if trainees are to produce,
as part of their course, magazines or other
literature for publication. Material with
a political or generally controversial
content should not be published.

Inclusion in the course of political and
related activities could be regarded as a
breach of your agreement with the MSC and
could result in the immediate closeure of
your course[7].

Apart from the issue of greater central
control, there are also indications that the
Manpower Services Commission's entry into this
area will have implications for the content and
orientation of education and training. The 1970s
saw a challenge to the traditional assumptions
about the aims and direction of education which
culminated in the "Great Debate" initiated in 1976
by the Prime Minister, James Callaghan. The
demand grew for more emphasis on basic skills and
greater attention to be paid to the "needs of
industry". The debate led to changes in the
traditional educational system but the most
radical changes were initiated not from within the
traditional system but from outside, by the Manpower Services Commission. The emphasis of the
Commission's initiatives has been on preparation
for work, not simply through instruction in
technical skills, but also through the development
of acceptable attitudes at work. In some ways
too great an emphasis on particular technical
skills has been seen as undesirable for in a
rapidly changing technological society particular
skills quickly become out of date. The emphasis
consequently has been much more on basic work
skills which facilitate flexibility and adapta-
bility.
The Manpower Services Commission, then,
through its developments in education and training

The Strategy and its Implications

has seized the initiative and put the traditional
educational system on the defensive. The value
of education in its own right increasingly has
been questioned: the value of education as a
preparation for work and as a way of meeting the
needs of industry has become widely accepted. In
practice, the implications for the control and
direction of education may be just as important a
consequence of the Manpower Services Commission's
policy measures on youth unemployment as anything
else.

Notes

1. Central Policy Review Staff, Education Training and Industrial Performance. HMSO,
   London, 1980, p.7. Quoted by D Finn, 'Whose
   Needs? Schooling and the "Needs" of Industry'
   in T L Rees, P Atkinson, Youth Unemployment
   and State Intervention, Routledge and Kegan
   Paul, London, 1982.
2. D Finn, 'The Youth Training Scheme - a New
   Deal?', Youth and Policy, Spring 1983, p.17.
3. G Markall, D Gregory, 'Who Cares? The MSC
   Interventionists: Full of Easter Promise', in
   T L Rees, P Atkinson, op cit, p.62.
4. Unemployment Unit Bulletin, October 1982.
5. G Markall, D Gregory, op cit, pp.60-1.
6. Times Educational Supplement, 'MSC threatens
   L.e.a.s. with rival technical school system',
   November 19th, 1982, pp.1 & 3.
7. C Waugh, 'Youth training scheme - in whose
   interests? - the coming struggle of the left',
   Socialism and Education, Vol 10, No.1, 1983,
   pp.2-3.

Chapter Eight

CONCLUSIONS

The reaction to the rise in the level of youth
unemployment in the mid 1970s was conditioned by
uncertainty about the likely duration of the
problem. Some commentators argued that the rise
in the level of unemployment in general and youth
unemployment in particular was the result of the
oil crisis of the early 1970s and would be short
lived. Although this view was by no means
universally held a case could be made to support
it. There had been frequent fluctuations in the
level of unemployment in earlier years and eventually it appeared that any rise was more or less
reversed. In chapter 2 it was seen that the
level of unemployment in general and youth unemployment in particular fell back in the late 1970s
and, superficially, this gave some reason to
believe that the pattern of earlier years would be
repeated. In practice, a more detailed analysis
of the unemployment figures already showed some
more worrying trends. The reverse in the rise in
unemployment levels was not as pronounced as the
movement it was correcting and it seemed as if
unemployment levels were gradually rising despite
cyclical movements which might mask the real
trend. Many commentators were arguing, therefore, in the mid 1970s, that the unemployment
problem was not short term, was not just linked to
the oil crisis, but was the reflection of deeper
seated structural changes. However, while this
view may have persuaded many it was not one that
was taken by government spokesmen. The policy of
the government, in particular in terms of special
employment measures, was clearly influenced by a
belief that the problems being faced largely were
short term.

Conclusions

While the kind of policy initiatives taken in the mid 1970s to deal with youth unemployment in part were influenced by official assumptions about the causes and duration of unemployment they were also in part influenced by the gathering consensus that what by then was seen as the traditional demand management response to a depression was no longer an acceptable policy option because of its inflationary dangers. Special employment measures were seen as having the minimum inflationary effect although some commentators pointed out that one could not assume that they would have a nil or even a negligible effect in this area. However, while these views about the duration and causes of unemployment, and the inflationary implications of the policy options, were important in determining the kind of initiatives taken they were less valuable in explaining the need to take an initiative of any kind in the first place.

Why, then, did the Labour Government of the mid 1970s feel the need to take special measures to deal with the rise in the level of youth unemployment? If the assumption was, as has been argued, that the rise was probably a temporary phenomenon, then why not simply let economic forces take their course? There are three main factors that help to explain why this line was not taken. First, there is no doubt that many who were able to influence the direction of policy were genuinely concerned by the impact of unemployment on the young people directly affected. In Chapter 1 it was noted that despite the cushion provided by state financial benefits and the help that may be available from family and friends, prolonged unemployment can create major financial problems. Further it was argued that the social consequences of prolonged unemployment can have, if anything, even more dramatic social and psychological consequences. In the discussion of the political debate surrounding the introduction of special employment measures it was pointed out that such problems were regularly highlighted, for example, in speeches in Parliament. The second factor, is that many of those able to influence policy seem to have been concerned about the consequences of prolonged high levels of youth unemployment for society at large. The links between unemployment on the one hand and crime and delinquency, social unrest, and 'unemployability' on the other were examined in Chapter 1

and the difficulty of establishing a firm view on
the strength and nature of the link between many
factors was highlighted. However, it was also
noted that what is important in this context is
not the balance of the academic debate but the
views held by those influential in policy making,
and the two need not necessarily be the same.
The third factor was the belief on the part of
policy makers that it was important for party
political reasons to be seen to be taking action
to deal with unemployment. In the case of the
Labour Government in power in the mid 1970s the
party political reasons were not simply related to
the impact of the high unemployment figures on
general public opinion, though this in itself was
important, but they were also related to the need
to maintain the social contract with the trade
unions.

The special employment measures introduced in
the mid 1970s ranged from job creation, to subsidies, to training, to efforts to reduce the size
of the active labour force. In many cases they
were prepared to meet an immediate emergency, in
some cases they were directly influenced by
similar measures elsewhere (as with the Job
Creation Programme) but more generally they were
experimental and initially seen as short term.
The evidence on the impact of these measures
reviewed in Chapter 6 suggests that they had
varying degrees of success. The subsidies were
possibly least successful in terms of their
explicit objectives and these were abandoned
fairly swiftly as a way of dealing with youth
unemployment by the Labour Government though they
were revived by later administrations. The job
creation measures provided short term employment
for increasing numbers of young people though
employment rates after leaving job creation
schemes varied: the post scheme employment rates
of Work Experience Programme participants were
relatively high but the rates for Job Creation
Programme Participants were less encouraging and
more generally it appeared that many who obtained
jobs after leaving a project were those who one
might have anticipated, on the basis of their
qualifications and previous employment history,
would do so.

The special employment measures developed by
Conservative governments since the 1979 General
Election have been introduced against a background

of a growing realisation that the problem being faced is at least a medium if not a long term phenomenon. In Chapter 2 it was noted that after the fall in the level of unemployment in general and the level of youth unemployment in particular in the late 1970s the trend has once again been reversed. Prediction of levels of unemployment from within academic and official circles and those made by international agencies like the OECD all assume that Britain will have to face levels of unemployment that are high by comparison with previous post Second World War experience, at least for the medium term future.

In the early years after the election of the Conservative Government in 1979 efforts were made to reduce reliance on special employment measures. The view that real jobs would only be created when the underlying economic ills were cured was frequently heard. However, later this position was reversed and the coverage of special employment measures has been extended.

There is no doubt that some of the factors that lay behind the previous Labour Government's decision to use special employment measures to try to control youth unemployment also influenced the Conservative administration. For example, the potential impact of high reported levels of unemployment on party political fortunes was keenly appreciated and there is an argument that had the 1979-83 administration not been able to persuade the electorate that its actions on unemployment were at least as effective as those likely to be taken by any competing party then it would not have been re-elected. On the other hand it appears that some of the other factors that lay behind the Labour Government's decisions to use special measures were not as widely held by those able to influence policy. For example, while there was a view that youth unemployment was a major economic and social disaster for those directly affected this view seemed to be tempered in some government circles by the belief that the unemployed must themselves share part of the blame for their plight. Similarly, while a number of Members of Parliament from the Government as well as from the opposition parties argued in debates that high levels of youth unemployment were a serious social threat and a potential cause of social unrest, by no means all influential figures took this view, and the Prime Minister argued that the impact of unemployment on the 1981 riots had been overstated.

Special employment measures, though, came to be seen even by those who were sceptical about some of the previously influential arguments, as valuable for other reasons. In particular they came to be seen as a way of influencing the attitudes of the young, and critically of influencing the direction of education and training. In the last chapter it was argued that one of the most important implications of the development of recent initiatives connected with youth unemployment has been the transfer of significant responsibility from the traditional education sector to a labour market agency, the Manpower Services Commission. There is little doubt that this implication was recognised by those responsible for policy on such matters and was one of the reasons for its attraction.

There has been a degree of continuity between the special employment measures used in the mid 1970s to combat the high level of youth unemployment and those used in the early 1980s. The continuity arises in the continued use of measures like job creation and attempts to reduce the size of the economically active labour force. Of course, there have been changes in the details of these measures and some of the earlier difficulties associated with what were then essentially emergency responses have been overcome. Other changes, particularly those associated with the introduction of the Community Programme, have been much more contentious. The real departure in terms of special employment measures, though, arises in the areas of job subsidy and training. Subsidies were abandoned by the Labour administration of the mid to late 1970s as a way of reducing the level of youth unemployment, largely because, as was argued in Chapter 6, research suggested that they were ineffective. They have been revived by the Conservative administration in a different form, centrally linked to low wage occupations. Training has been on the political agenda for many years but the initiative taken by the Conservative Government in the early 1980s marks a radical departure. It marks a departure in terms both of the balance of special employment measures (it is now much more clearly the case that training rather than job creation is seen as the relevant response for the under 18 year olds)

and as has been argued earlier, it marks a departure in the way in which it has tried to make the
exercise much more directly relevant to the needs
of industry.

The research evidence on the extent to which
these more recent special employment measures have
met their objectives is necessarily not as comprehensive. Nevertheless there are some indications
of the performance of certain of them. For
example, it appears as if job subsidies of the
1980s have faced much the same problems as their
predecessors of the mid 1970s. In particular, it
appears as if only a relatively small number of
really new jobs have been created. There is no
research evidence on the impact of the subsidies
on wage levels though many believe that the Young
Workers Scheme has more closely met its objectives
in this area. Similarly, the difficulties faced
by many leaving job creation programmes, which
began to be seen at the end of the 1970s appear to
have intensified in recent years. Post-scheme
employment rates are now very low and it appears
as if for many young people job creation is simply
an interlude in a period of prolonged unemployment. This is clearly not universally the case,
but it has been argued that to the extent that it
is the case it is a cause for concern. The evidence quoted earlier suggests that the positive
social/psychological benefits of engagement on a
job creation project will be lost if a job is not
found fairly quickly after leaving a scheme.
Further, it has been argued that if a job is not
found after leaving a job creation project not
only may the positive benefit of working on that
project be lost, but there may also well be
negative consequences (such as an increase in the
cynicism felt about the motives of those supporting the schemes and a reinforcing of the view
that there is little that can be done to meet the
problems young people face within the confines of
the present political system). Some success has
been claimed for the Youth Training Scheme in at
least one respect. Despite fears that there
would be a significant shortage of places the
number provided has been reasonably close to the
target. However the distribution of places and
their overall quality is contentious. Many
trainees are retained by scheme sponsors after
completion of training but this only serves to
reinforce doubts about the extent to which youth

training is being used as a substitution for
normal employment.

The special employment measures of the early
1980s have been introduced on the basis of assumptions about the causes of unemployment that were
not widely held in the mid 1970s. The assumptions that high levels of youth unemployment in
large part are the result of high levels of young
people's wages and the lack of preparation offered
in the traditional education sector for the world
of work were held by some in the 1970s but have
become much more influential with policy makers in
the early 1980s. Some of the initiatives, like
job subsidies and youth training, clearly are
predicated on these assumptions. However, it
has been suggested that the balance of argument is
that these factors have been far less influential
than is assumed. Much more important, as a cause
of youth unemployment, has been the general level
of economic activity. If this view is correct
then one can expect that the range of special
employment measures introduced in the early 1980s
will do little to alleviate the problems caused by
high levels of youth unemployment. Of course,
this does not mean that they will not have, as has
been argued, a siginficant impact in other areas
such as the content and direction of education and
training in Britain, nor does it not mean that
they will not serve other political purposes.

Atkinson A B & Fleming J S (1978) 'Unemployment,
    social security and incentives', Midland Bank
    Review, Autumn
Banks M & Jackson P R (1982) 'Unemployment and the
    risk of minor psychiatric disorder in young
    people: cross sectional and longitudinal
    evidence', Psychological Medicine, No 12,
    pp 789-798
Banks M H, Mullings C & Jackson E J (1983)
    'A bench mark for youth opportunities',
    Employment Gazette, March, pp 91-5
Baxter J C (1975) 'The chronic job changer:
    A study of youth unemployment', Social and
    Economic Administration, Vol 9, No 3
Bedeman T & Courtney G (1982) 'Taking the
    opportunity', Employment Gazette, October
Bedeman T & Harvey J (1982) Young People on YOP -
    A National Survey of Entrants to the Youth
    Opportunites Programme, MSC, London, Research
    and Development Series No 3
Brennan M E & Lancashire R (1978) 'Associations of
    childhood mortality with housing status and
    unemployment', Journal of Epidemiology and
    Community Health, Vol 32, No 1, pp 28-33
Brennan M E (1978) 'Patterns of mortality and the
    alienation of life: A study using census
    indicators' in Armytage W H C & Peel J (eds)
    Perimiters of Social Despair, Academic Press
    London, pp 73-9
Brennan M E (1979) 'Mortality and the national
    economy: A review of experience in England and
    Wales 1936-76', Lancet, 15 September, pp 568-73
Campbell M & Jones D (1982) 'Racial discrimination
    against Asian school leavers', Unemployment
    Unit Bulletin, No 5, October, pp 4-5

Bibliography

Casson M (1979) <u>Youth Unemployment</u>, Macmillan,
    London
Carr-Hill R A & Stern N H (1979) <u>Crime, the Police
    and Criminal Statistics</u>, Academic Press, London
Carr-Hill R A & Stern N H (1983) 'Crime, unemploy-
    ment and the police', <u>Research Note No. 2,
    SSRC Programme on Taxation, Incentives and the
    Distribution of Income</u>, International Centre
    for Economics and Related Disciplines, London
    School of Economics and Political Science
Carr-Hill R A & Stern N H (1983) 'Unemployment and
    crime: A comment', <u>Journal of Social Policy</u>,
    Vol 12, Part 3
Central Advisory Council for Education, (1959)
    <u>15-18</u>, HMSO London
Central Policy Review Staff (1980) <u>Education,
    Training and Industrial Performance</u>, HMSO,
    London
Cherry N (1976) 'Persistent job changing - is it a
    problem?', <u>Journal of Occupational Psychology</u>
Clark K B & Summers L H (1980) 'The dynamics of
    youth unemployment' in Freeman R B & Wise D
    (eds) National Bureau of Economic Research
    Conference on Youth Unemployment
Colledge M & Bartholomew R (1980) 'The long-term
    unemployed: Some new evidence', <u>Employment
    Gazette</u>, January, p 11
Crow I (1982) 'The unemployment/crime link',
    <u>Unemployment Unit Bulletin</u>, No 4
Davies L, Bedeman T & Harvey S (1982) 'What
    happens after YOP - a longer term view',
    <u>Employment Gazette</u>, January, pp 12-14
Davies B, Hamill L, Moylan S & Smee C H (1982)
    'Incomes in and out of work', <u>Employment
    Gazette</u>, June
Department of Employment (1981) <u>A New Training
    Initiative: A Programme for Action</u>, HMSO,
    London, Cmnd 8455
Dex S (1979) 'A note on discrimination in
    employment and its effects on black youths',
    <u>Journal of Social Policy</u>, Vol 8, No 3,
    pp 357-69
Dowes R E & Hughes J (1976) 'The family, the
    school and the political socialisation
    process' in Rose R (ed) <u>Studies in British
    Politics</u>, Macmillan, London (3rd edition)
Eisenbert P & Lazarfeld P F (1933) 'The psycho-
    logical effects of unemployment',
    <u>Psychological Bulletin</u>

Bibliography

Employment Gazette (1984) 'Unemployment and ethnic
    origin', June pp 260-264
Faulkner M (1978) Direct Job Creation in the Member
    State of the European Community, EEC, Brussels,
    Study No 77/15
Feldstein M (1973) Lowering the Permanent Rate of
    Unemployment, US Congress, Joint Economic
    Committee, Washington, USA
Finn D (1982) 'Whose needs? Schooling and the
    "needs" of industry'in Rees T L & Atkinson P,
    Youth Unemployment and State Intervention,
    Routledge & Kegan Paul, London
Finn D (1983) 'The Youth Training Scheme - a new
    deal?' Youth and Policy, Spring
Fleisher B M (1963) 'The effects of unemployment
    on juvenile delinquency', Journal of Political
    Economy, Vol 71
Francis L (1982) Youth in Transit, Gower, Aldershot
Gardner M J et al (1969) 'Patterns of mortality in
    middle and early old age in the county bor-
    oughs of England and Wales', British Journal
    of Preventative and Social Medicine, Vol 23,
    pp 133-40
Gurney M (1980) 'The effects of unemployment on
    the psycho-social development of school
    leavers', Occupational Psychology, Vol 53,
    pp 205-13
Hakim C (1982)'The social consequences of high
    unemployment', Journal of Social Policy, Vol
    11, Part 4
Higgins J (1978) The Poverty Business: Britain and
    America, Basil Blackwell/Martin Robertson,
    Oxford
Higgins J (1980) 'Social control theories of
    social policy", Journal of Social Policy,
    Vol 9, No 11, pp 1-23
Home Office, (1981) The Brixton Disorders 10-12
    April, 1981 Report on an Inquiry by the Rt Hon
    Lord Scarman, OBE, HMSO, London Cmnd 8427
Hyman H (1959) Political Socialisation, Free Press
    New York
Jackson M P & Hanby V J B (1982) British Work
    Creation Programmes, Gower, Aldershot
Jaffe R & Froomkin J (1978) 'Occupational oppor-
    tunities for college education workers,
    1950-1975', Monthly Labour Review, June
Johnson C C & Tunda J Q (1974) An Impact
    Evaluation of the Public Employment Program,
    US Department of Labor, Office of Assistant

Secretary for Policy Evaluation and Research, Washington

Jones P (1983) 'Effects of rising unemployment on school leavers', Employment Gazette, January, pp 13-16

Karsten D (1980) Job Creation schemes in the European Community, EEC, Brussels, Study No 80/40

Kavanagh D (1972) Political Culture, Macmillan, London

Little C R, Villemez W J & Smith D A (1982) 'One step forward, two steps back: more on the class/criminality controversy', American Sociological Review, June, Vol 47, No 3, pp 435-8

Lynch L (1983) Job Search and Youth Unemployment Centre for Labour Economics Discussion Paper, No 158

Lynch L N & Richardson R (1982) 'Unemployment of Young Workers in Britain', British Journal of Industrial Relations, Vol XX, No 3 November

Maddison A (1980) 'Measuring labour-slack', Employment Gazette, July, pp 727-33

Makeham P (1980) Youth Unemployment, Department of Employment Research Paper No 10, HMSO, London

Maki D & Spindler Z A (1975) 'The Effect of Unemployment Compensation on the Rate of Unemployment in Great Britain', Oxford Economic Papers, Vol 27, November

Manpower Services Commission (1978) Young People and Work, Manpower Studies No 19781, HMSO, London

Markall G & Gregory D (1982) 'Who cares? The MSC intervenes. Full of Easter promise', in Rees R & Atkinson P, Youth Unemployment and State Intervention, Routledge & Kegan Paul, London

Marsden D & Duff E (1975) Workless - Some Unemployed Men and their Families. Penguin, Harmondsworth

Martin J (1983) Effects of the Minimum Wage on the Youth Labour Market in North America and France, OECD, Occasional Studies

Melvyn P (1977) Youth Unemployment: Roots and Remedies, World Employment Programme research, Working Paper, ILO, Geneva

Merrilees W & Wilson R (1979) Disequilibrium in the Labour Market for Young People in Great Britain, Manpower Research Group Discussion Paper No 10, Warwick University

Bibliography

Miller J (1982) Situation Vacant, Community
    Projects Foundation, London
Mishra R (1981) Society and Social Policy:
    Theoretical Perspective on Welfare, Macmillan,
    London
Moon J (1984) 'The responses of British governments
    to unemployment' in Richardon J & Henning R,
    Unemployment: Policy Responses of Western
    Democracies, Sage, London
Mungham G (1982) 'Workless youth as a moral panic'
    in Rees R L & Atkinson P, Youth Unemployment
    and State Intervention, Routledge & Kegan
    Paul, London, pp 38-9
National Youth Employment Council (1974)
    Unqualified, Untrained and Unemployed, HMSO,
    London
Nickell S (1979) 'The effect of unemployment and
    related benefits on the duration of
    unemployment', Economic Journal, Vol 89
O'Connor D (1982) 'Probabilities of employment
    after work experience', Employment Gazette,
    January, pp 8-11
Organisation for Economic Co-operation and
    Development (1978) Youth Unemployment, Vol 1,
    OECD, Paris
Organisation for Economic Co-operation and
    Development (1980) Youth Unemployment: The
    Causes and Consequences, OECD, Paris
Pahl R E (1982) 'Family, community and unemploy-
    ment', New Society, 21 January, pp 91-93
Phillips L, Votey H L & Maxwell P (1972),
    'Crime, youth and the labour market', Journal
    of Political Economy, Vol 80, No 3
Ramsden S & Smee C (1981) 'The health of unem-
    ployed men, DHSS cohort study', Employment
    Gazette, September pp 397-401
Raffe D (1983) 'Youth unemployment and the MSC:
    1977-1983' in McClone D, The Scottish Govern-
    ment Yearbook 1984, Unit for the Study of
    Government in Scotland, Edinburgh
Report from the Select Committee of the House of
    Lords on Unemployment, Vol 1, HMSO, London
Ridley F F (1981) 'View from a disaster area:
    unemployed youth in Merseyside' in Crick B
    (ed) Unemployment, Methuen, London
Roberts K, Duggan J & Noble M (1981) 'Ignoring the
    signs: young, unemployed and unregistered',
    Employment Gazette, August, pp 353-6
Rousselet J et al (1975) Les jeunes et l'emploi,
    Presses Universitaires de France, Paris

Bibliography

Sears D O (1975) 'Political socialisation' in
    Greenstein F I & Polsbyn N, Micropolitical
    Theory, Addison Wesley, New York, pp 93-154
Sears D O & McConahay J B (1973) The Politics of
    Violence, Houghton Mifflin, Boston
Sinfield A (1971) 'Poor and out-of-work in Shields'
    in Townsend P (ed) The Concept of Poverty,
    Heinemann, London, p 228
Sinfield A (1981) What Unemployment Means, Martin
    Robertson, Oxford
Showler B (1981) 'Political economy and unemploy-
    ment' in Showler B & Sinfield A (eds), The
    Workless State, Martin Robertson, Oxford,
    pp 27-58
Smith D J (1980) 'Unemployment and racial minority
    groups', Employment Gazette, June, pp 602-6
Sorrentino C (1981) 'Unemployment in international
    perspective' in Showler B & Sinfield A, The
    Workless State, Martin Robertson, Oxford
Stafford C H (1982) 'The impact of the Youth
    Opportunities Programme on young people's
    employment prospects and psychological well
    being', British Journal of Guidance and
    Counselling, Vol 10, pp 12-21
Stafford E M , Jackson P R & Banks M H (1980)
    'Employment, work involvement and mental
    illness in less qualified young people',
    Journal of Occupational Psychology, Vol 53, pp
    291-304
Stevens P & Willis C F (1979) Race, Crime and
    Arrests, Home Office Research Study No 58,
    HMSO, London
Stokes G (1981) Unemployment Among School Leavers,
    University of Birmingham (mimeo)
Taylor R (1978) Labour and the Social Contract,
    Fabian Tract, 458, Civil Press, Glasgow
Times Educational Supplement (1982) 'MSC threatens
    L.e.a.s. with rival technical school system',
    November pp 1 & 3
Waugh C (1983) 'Youth training scheme - in whose
    interests? - the coming struggle of the left',
    Socialism and Education, Vol 10, No 1, pp 2-3
Wells W (1983) The Relative Pay and Employment of
    Young People, Research Paper No 42, Department
    of Employment
Willis P G (1977) Learning to Labour, Saxon House,
    Farnborough
Youthaid (1981) Quality or Collapse? Youthaid
    Review of the Youth Opportunities Programme,
    Youthaid, London

Index

Index